D.I.Y.
DELICIOUS

D.I.Y. DELICIOUS

Recipes and Ideas for
Simple Food from Scratch

by
VANESSA BARRINGTON

Photographs by
SARA REMINGTON

CHRONICLE BOOKS
SAN FRANCISCO

Library of Congress Cataloging-in-Publication Data available.
ISBN: 978-0-8118-7346-8

Manufactured in China

Designed by Suzanne LaGasa
Prop styling by Kami Bremyer
Food styling by Nani (Romney) Steele
Typesetting by Janis Reed
Page 28: *Premonitions of Flynn for Vanessa* by Susan Fleming, 2001

10 9 8 7 6 5 4 3 2 1

Chronicle Books LLC
680 Second Street
San Francisco, California 94107
www.chroniclebooks.com

Maseca is a registered trademark of Maseca or GRUMA, S.A.B. de C.V.;
Microplane is a registered trademark of Grace Manufacturing, Inc.; Crock-Pot
is a registered trademark of Sunbeam Products, Inc.; Guss's Pickles is a
registered trademark of Crossing Delancey Pickle Enterprises Corporation;
iPhone is a registered trademark of Apple Inc.; Lodge is a registered trademark
of Lodge Manufacturing Company; eBay is a registered trademark of eBay Inc.;
Amazon is a registered trademark of Amazon.com, Inc.; Maytag blue cheese
is a registered trademark of Maytag Dairy Farms; Artisana is a registered
trademark of Artisana Raw Organic Nut Butter; Exo Superpeel is a registered
trademark of ExoProducts, Inc.

*This book is dedicated to every eater
and cook who has ever asked the question,
"Why can't I make this myself?"*

CONTENTS

INTRODUCTION

The Resourceful Kitchen

A few years ago, while attending a family reunion, I visited the house my mother grew up in during the 1930s. The low-slung, brown, brick house sits on a large lot on the outskirts of a small town near Salt Lake City. The house was surrounded by a farm until a portion of the property was sold to the high school next door. My mother's siblings, Aunt Amelia (Aunt Mil) and Uncle Don, still live there. They still grow a few rows of this and that, and the crabapple tree still bears fruit. The pantry off the kitchen was the thing that struck me most powerfully. The shelves were lined with pickles, preserves, jams, jellies, and canned tomatoes and other vegetables from the garden. It looked strangely foreign to me, like a museum in some other country.

My mom never canned or preserved a thing. She relied on packaged, convenience products to put dinner on the table seven days a week while working a nine-to-five job. Cooking was work. The only time she seemed to enjoy cooking was on special occasions when she'd make some of our traditional Serbian family dishes: sarma (stuffed cabbage rolls) or the yeasted, barely sweet walnut-date bread called *orevnitza* that's only served at Christmastime, or Aunt Mil's jam-filled sugar cookies. Today, I'm thankful that Aunt Mil stayed in that house all these years, preserving the harvest right along with our family food traditions.

When I first saw all those jars neatly lined up, their contents barely discernible in the dim light, the hand-written labels indecipherable, I felt both happy and a little wistful. Happy they were there, but wistful because something that should have been part of me wasn't. I'd missed out on a culinary tradition. That was when the memories of eating at my grandmother's house came back—dim ones to be sure. I was only four when we moved away to California. But I do remember platters of homemade food full of richness, love, and skill. I remember women working in the kitchen. I remember playing outside between the rows of plants. I remember the first time I learned what a honeysuckle tasted like.

By the time of that family reunion, I was already a professional cook with a natural curiosity about how things work in the kitchen. Still, I wasn't as connected to my food as I wanted to be. After seeing my mom's family home, I went back to my home inspired because I knew that those Depression-era characteristics were in my genes—resourcefulness and an inability to waste food.

BEYOND THE PACKAGE

My personal journey into making more of my own basic foods started as a way to revive the lost kitchen arts that I had seen my aunt upholding. I questioned why I was purchasing everyday staples that are so easy to make—things like granola, bread, butter, tortillas, and pickles. I started dabbling a little here and there, noticing how much better most anything I made from scratch tasted than any food from a package—however special or gourmet it purported to be. I began looking at labels more closely, noticing the ingredients that are added to almost all foods to preserve their shelf life, color, and texture. I knew that even the highest-quality products weren't necessarily made with the freshest, tastiest, seasonal produce, because they're made year-round, not just when the ingredients are at their best. Packaged foods have to be consistent and cost effective. Seasonality isn't a consideration. I wanted to get beyond the packaging altogether and create a completely homemade kitchen.

That was about the time I realized I was drowning in plastic quart containers from my daily yogurt habit. It made me a little sick just to think about all that plastic—not just what I was buying, but what others discarded as well. I wondered if it was really necessary. I considered buying a yogurt maker but visions of abandoned appliances left on urban sidewalks stopped me: Those sad, yellowed yogurt makers, Crock-Pots, and bread machines left over after yard sales with hastily scrawled signs saying "FREE" taped onto them. I thought, "Do I really need another appliance?" Surely people made yogurt successfully before there were yogurt makers. So I did some research and figured out that all you really need is a way to keep the milk warm while it cultures. I looked at many suggestions and rigged up a method that worked for me.

Another thing happened that pushed me even farther away from packaged foods. One summer Sunday, I noticed that a family member's backyard plum tree was literally dripping with gorgeous, plump, purple plums. After gorging ourselves on several, we realized that the bulk of the remainder needed to be harvested that day or they would end up falling to the ground and rotting. Yet, I could easily imagine any of us in a grocery store buying jam within the next few weeks. It seemed criminal. We got out the ladder and worked together filling countless paper grocery bags. We gave away all we could to friends, neighbors, and a local foraging group called Forage Oakland; ate more than we should; froze all that would fit in the freezer; and still there were more. The next day I made jam for the first time. The family got their plums back in jars. They were delighted. I brought some to friends. We ate it all winter on toast and stirred into yogurt. Many people told me it was the best jam they'd ever had. I thought so, too. I came to a realization: If I can make the best jam ever on the first try, in just a couple of hours, why buy it? If you truly care how your food tastes and about knowing exactly what's in it, why buy anything when you can make it yourself?

Around this time, a lot was happening outside of my kitchen. Just as the Slow Food movement was starting to penetrate beyond its early adherents, and more people were becoming aware of the pleasures of eating locally and simply, people started waking up to the problems in our industrialized, globalized food system. It was becoming clear that our food is making us sick—sometimes very slowly, through unhealthful additives and the wrong kinds of calories. And sometimes more quickly, through food contamination and adulteration. Then the economy started to shake and food prices climbed suddenly. Feelings of vulnerability sparked a nationwide resurgence in self-reliance activities not seen since World War II—activities like urban farming, suburban homesteading, keeping chickens, foraging, canning, preserving, and planting backyard gardens. It seemed that just as people were finding that they wanted to reconnect with their food, they were learning that they might just have to.

The truth is, we're not very handy in the kitchen anymore. We're accustomed to convenience and being able to buy whatever we need whenever we need it. For many people who do cook, spending time in the kitchen has become a recreational weekend activity, not an everyday way of feeding ourselves. Even those of us who cook every day sometimes struggle with putting dinner on the table night after night, and a lot of us resort to take-out more than we'd like.

I like knowing that I have the skills to make something I could easily buy. It's important to me to have food on hand that I've made myself because then I always have the makings of a meal. When there are pickles, sauerkraut, bread (either fresh or in the freezer), salad dressing, cheese, eggs, and a few vegetables in my larder, I'm in control of what I'm eating that day. I don't have to be at the mercy of the grocery store deli when I'm tired. Or go out when I'd rather be home. Or spend money I'd rather save. Or eat something that's neither healthful nor tasty. Instead of feeling frustrated, stressed, and out of control, I feel resourceful and ready for anything. I feel like I'm taking good care of myself and my loved ones. Just as the victory gardens planted during the World Wars made people more self-reliant, my well-stocked kitchen and new way of eating is like a personal victory over the chaos of life.

That's what I want to share with you—more than just a collection of recipes, but a way of eating that is uncomplicated, sensible, and at the same time, deeply satisfying. I didn't invent many of the techniques in this book. Yogurt, sauerkraut, sourdough bread, and fresh cheese existed long before me, but I've put my own twist on them and put them together into one book. I hope the foods in this book will serve as building blocks for your own new way of eating. You'll also find recipes that utilize one or more of the basic food items as a way to demonstrate how you can use the building blocks. There are special sections with ideas for easy meal preparation that I hope will help you eat better and inspire your own ideas. And, of course, you don't have to make everything yourself. Start with a few items that inspire you and you'll begin to see how you can combine homemade items with store-bought ones, as well as fresh meats and produce, and you'll likely find yourself building a repertoire of homemade foods over time.

I hope this book will help you integrate the preparation of food into your daily experience, slow down, and enjoy cooking and mealtimes more. I hope it will inspire you to reconnect with both your food and the people with whom you eat. I hope you feel proud of the things you make with your own hands and that you enjoy them deeply.

Special Processes and Techniques

This book includes a variety of different types of recipes, with varying levels of complexity. At its most simple, there's a repertoire of basic salad dressings to serve as a reminder that salad dressings don't have to come in bottles. You'll find two salsa recipes that are easier, yet much tastier, than anything you'll find in a store. Slightly more complex, but easier than you probably think, are items like homemade crackers, jam, tortillas, and mustard.

There are a few techniques that may be new to you. They were once new to me, too, and I was apprehensive. Don't worry; we're in this together! I consulted experts for several areas of this book in which I wasn't an expert, and I encourage you to do the same in your communities and families. Skill sharing is a great way to build community and self-reliance.

As you learn new skills, you'll find that an understanding of how things work in the kitchen not only increases your self-reliance, but it also bolsters your connection to the natural and scientific worlds. All human cultures once knew that salt and wild bacterial organisms that live in our environment could be used to preserve vegetables, resulting in healthful, delicious foods like sauerkraut and kimchi. Scalding milk and then inoculating it with the proper bacteria to make yogurt is an easy process but seems magical the first time you do it. Teaching yourself and your children the science of the kitchen can not only be fun, but it can provide a great sense of satisfaction.

FERMENTATION

Fermentation is one of the special techniques here that may be new to you. The surprising list of fermented foods we eat every day is exhaustive. Some of my favorite foods, such as salami, wine, cheese, and chocolate, are all products of fermentation. In this book, you'll learn how to make your own sourdough starter from scratch, using just the wild organisms in the air; red wine vinegar and kombucha from a special culture; sauerkraut, kimchi, and Wild Salvadoran Curtido by adding salt to inhibit harmful bacteria; and naturally carbonated soft drinks.

FEAR OF FERMENTATION: We tend to fear the things we don't understand, whether they are unfamiliar religions, cultures, or the workings of the internal combustion engine. Our disconnection from food likewise breeds a fear of unfamiliar kitchen processes. For example, many people are nervous the first few times they leave a food product out at room temperature for several days to let it ferment. That's a normal and reasonable reaction. Our modern food system has taught us to treat our foods like biohazards, because many of them are. Due to lack of traceability and proper inspection and enforcement protocols, the onus has been put on us to overcook our meat and bleach our countertops, because the food system can't guarantee that the foods we eat are safe. So, if you're worried about making yourself sick with fermented foods, consider that the government-supervised food system hasn't done such a good job of keeping us safe. Trust your own kitchen and your own judgment and senses. Keep things clean and pay attention to what your eyes and your nose tell you and you won't have any trouble.

If you're still nervous, remember that fermentation was developed as a way to preserve foods before refrigeration, and we somehow survived as people long enough to invent refrigerators. Fermentation occurs when beneficial bacteria and wild yeasts colonize food. Once the good bacteria colonize a food item, the bad bacteria don't stand a chance. On occasion, bad organisms get into a food before good ones—usually early in the process. That's why it's important to keep things clean. If it happens, you will know it. Your nose will tell you in no uncertain terms. I can't stress it enough. Trust yourself.

PICKLING

There are books on fermenting and there are books on canning and pickling. Usually, however, they are not the same books. I like fermented pickles, but I also like the bite of a nice vinegary pickled vegetable, so I've included both in this book. Pickling is easy. You just have to use the proper proportion of vinegar to keep it safe. I don't have a large garden, so I rarely find myself with a windfall of vegetables to preserve. The recipes in this book are for small batches of pickles that are kept in the refrigerator. However, I'm all for preserving and canning. If you are too, you likely already have a canning book. You can take the recipes in this book and scale them up and process them according to the canning chart in any recently updated canning book (see page 229). The U.S. Department of Agriculture (USDA) recommends canned processing for anything that will be stored at room temperature, including fermented pickles and jams.

CULTURING

There are several cultured dairy products in this book, including butter, yogurt, crème fraîche, and mascarpone. The culturing process is similar to fermentation. A culturing agent is introduced into either milk or cream, which is then exposed to the proper temperature conditions for the proper amount of time to allow the culturing agent to work. It's pretty much as simple as that. This process, like fermentation, tends to make people nervous. If anything, dairy products are even more likely than vegetables to tell you when something has gone wrong. So trust your nose.

Special Equipment

Is the D.I.Y. kitchen also an unplugged kitchen? Yes and no. I firmly believe that a person can successfully make bread without a bread maker and yogurt without a yogurt maker. And I do have a special relationship with the mortar and pestle on my counter. So in these senses, the D.I.Y. kitchen is unplugged.

On the other hand, both your blender and your food processor will get a pretty good workout in this book. The better the quality of these two pieces of equipment, the better the recipes will turn out. I also enjoy having a coffee grinder devoted to spices because it speeds things up, but a mortar and pestle work fine.

CAST IRON

A cast-iron skillet is one of the best pieces of kitchen equipment you will ever buy. Once it's well seasoned, it's like a trustworthy friend. It goes from the stove to the oven, nothing will stick to it, it cleans up like a dream, it browns and caramelizes like nobody's business, it makes perfect pancakes and tortillas, and it dry roasts the ingredients for authentic salsa better than anything else. And guess what? It's cheap. I've found great cast-iron skillets at garage sales for as little as $1 or $2 and even brand new, they won't set you back much. They're even still made in the United States. Get yourself one (see page 226).

MISCELLANEOUS TOOLS

You will need a few really good strainers for various recipes, both fine and medium mesh. A Crock-Pot or slow cooker is nice to have, and if you want to make corn tortillas, it's best to use a tortilla press. Of course, some tortillas are still made entirely by hand, but this is after years of daily practice. I believe in avoiding frustration in the kitchen as much as possible. A mortar and pestle are essential for pounding garlic into a paste for certain recipes in this book. It mellows the garlic and is used when you want the flavor of garlic to permeate a dish subtly but completely. It's a technique that is easy and quick, and when it's called for in a dish, it matters. A pasta maker is nice to have for homemade pasta, but it's not essential. For vinegar, you'll need some sort of crock, and for pizza, you'll be a very happy pizza maker indeed if you have a stone and a peel. All of these items are discussed in recipe head notes and the Sources and Further Reading section.

MASON JARS

You will need mason jars, mostly 1-quart, wide-mouthed jars, for many of the pickles and fermented items. These are also good for storing grains, granola, and leftovers. For jam, you'll want to buy smaller ones.

Ingredients

Kosher salt is used in almost all of the recipes in this book. It's a good all-purpose salt that is affordable and readily available. In cases where it might be nice to use a fancier salt, like a *fleur de sel,* I point it out, but it's never necessary. In cases where the directions say "season with salt," it isn't important what kind of salt you use. But for pickling and fermenting, it is important to use what's specified because different salts have different-sized crystals and they will tend to weigh and measure differently. For example, you must use about 50 percent more kosher salt in a recipe than pickling salt because pickling salt is finer grained.

I prefer to use organic turbinado sugar rather than bleached white sugar, simply because it's less processed. I buy organic because I think it's important to support organic practices, but it's not necessary for the recipes. Many of the recipes here call for alternative sweeteners like honey, agave syrup, or maple syrup.

A few special cultures are called for in this book to make dairy products, soft drinks, vinegar, and kombucha. Availability and sources are discussed in recipe head notes and also in the Sources section. Most of the spices used in this book are easy to find in regular stores across the country. A few items, such as Korean and Aleppo pepper, are found only in specialty or culturally specific food stores. For those items, substitutions are suggested, or look in the Sources section.

A Quick and Easy Guide to Homemade Foods

Besides the obvious benefits of eating more healthfully, and avoiding additives and excessive packaging, investing time in making foods from scratch can actually save you shopping and cooking time later on. You'll be surprised at how many creative ways you can use and repurpose the homemade foods in this book for quick, economical, and creative meals and snacks. The simplest things taste better because you've made them yourself!

Following are a few easy ideas for using various homemade foods to make impromptu appetizers and quick meals.

AJVAR (PAGE 74)

Serve with homemade or store-bought crackers or breads along with olives and homemade pickles for a quick and easy appetizer.

Whisk with olive oil and make a quick dressing for salads or drizzle over grilled or baked fish, chicken, or roasted potatoes.

Thin with a little white wine and use it to marinate fish just before cooking.

Stir into scrambled eggs during the last few minutes of cooking.

Use it as a pasta sauce or pizza topping.

SIMPLE WILD SAUERKRAUT (PAGE 186)

Serve alongside mashed potatoes and browned sausage.

Tuck into a grilled cheese sandwich with homemade or store-bought bread.

continued...

Toss with whole-wheat pasta and leftover Mustard and Bourbon–Glazed Pork Roast (page 36).

Eat with beans or atop a bean soup.

AVOCADO-TOMATILLO SALSA OR (PAGE 71) SIMPLE TOMATO SALSA (PAGE 72)

Smash some cooked pinto beans and make a layered dip with the beans and homemade Crème Fraîche (page 116) or store-bought sour cream.

Shred leftover chicken, beef, or pork and reheat with either type of salsa. Serve tucked into Tortillas.

Stir into scrambled eggs or homemade savory porridge served with an egg.

ALL-PURPOSE RED CHILI SAUCE (PAGE 70)

Stir into cooked beans and serve alongside rice or with eggs and tortillas.

Reheat leftover shredded chicken in the sauce for a mole-like dish.

Stir into cooked polenta or other porridge during the last few minutes of cooking and top with shredded cheese.

YOGURT (PAGE 98)

Drain for two hours and make a marinade for chicken or fish by adding lots of garlic, lemon juice, fresh herbs, and/or dried spices and a little olive oil.

Drizzle over cooked lentils or beans.

Stir into homemade porridge.

CREAMY HERB DRESSING (PAGE 81)

Repurpose it into a dip by draining it in cheesecloth over a bowl or sink for several hours.

CRÈME FRAÎCHE (PAGE 116)

Drizzle over fresh pasta or any vegetable soup.

Instead of cream, add it to a pasta dish or pureed soup during the last few minutes of cooking.

Serve with fresh fruit for dessert, drizzled with honey or not.

Drizzle over a pizza topped with smoked fish.

GARLICKY CUCUMBER PICKLE RELISH (PAGE 208)

Serve on a pork or chicken sandwich.

Drain well and sprinkle over a cured meat or smoked fish pizza after it comes out of the oven.

Serve on crackers with soft cheese.

Serve with beans.

SPICY KIMCHI (PAGE 191)

Add to grain salads.

Enjoy alongside brown rice and canned sardines, herring, or mackerel.

Toss with soba noodles and vegetables.

D.I.Y. BABY FOOD

If you don't eat processed food, why should your baby? Commercial baby food in little jars is a convenience to be sure. Those little jars are super-portable. But they are expensive, and what's on the ingredients list? Even if there are no additives on the list, how can you know that the best-tasting and freshest ingredients went into that jar? The best way to teach kids to like vegetables and other good-for-you foods is to make sure that the first such foods they try taste great. Not to mention, those little jars are a waste of production energy even if they do go in the recycling.

It's easy and fast to make your own baby food and it can be just as convenient to store and transport as little jars. The best way is to freeze portions of homemade baby food in ice cube trays and then store them in resealable plastic bags. When you need food to go, take out a few cubes; transfer them to a small, lidded container; and tuck it into an insulated bag. The food will thaw while you're out and about.

Baby food can be any kind of real food, as long as allergies are taken into account and it's not heavily seasoned. You'll want to balance the fruits, vegetables, grains, and proteins. In many cases, baby can eat the same thing you're eating, sometimes with textural adjustments, sometimes not. Whole-grain porridge (see page 179) is a good example of a baby-ready food.

FRUITS: apples, peaches, pears, melons, berries, citrus

VEGETABLES: green beans, peas, legumes, squash, root vegetables, broccoli, greens, corn

GRAINS: brown rice, oats, barley, farro, porridge

PROTEINS: small portions of meat, plain Yogurt (page 98), Fresh Whole-Milk Soft Cheese (page 106)

There are books and Web sites that detail how to make baby food, but all you really need to do to any of the previously listed foods is to cook (in most cases), mash or puree, and store properly.

COOKING METHODS: steam, roast, or boil

PUREEING METHODS: blender, food processor, immersion blender, potato masher, baby food mill

STORAGE: ice cube trays; resealable plastic bags; small, portable lidded containers

D.I.Y. PET FOOD

Even before the problems with deadly contaminants in pet food surfaced, many pet owners questioned whether commercial pet food was really the best thing for their beloved family members. Even if you buy a respected brand of organic pet food in a pet store, you're still getting highly processed food, akin to some of the organic packaged and processed foods on the market today, only with more by-products. As with any processed food, you're really buying convenience. It's important to remember that domestic animals evolved by living alongside humans and eating most of the same foods humans ate, in the form of table scraps.

I'm not suggesting you feed your pet only table scraps, but in some cases it's a fine idea. Brown rice or other grains, with a little broth and some vegetables from a soup are perfectly good foods for your dog. I often feed my dog foods that I cannot use or don't want to eat (but that aren't spoiled)—it's better than wasting food. Ground-up fish bones or cooked soup bones are also good for dogs, and a treat they'll appreciate. Trimmings from fish or fresh meats are other good candidates.

Since you can't count on your table scraps to feed your dog or cat, there are other ways to go about making sure your animals have the healthiest food possible.

Before making drastic changes in your pet's menu, I recommend speaking to your veterinarian and doing some research. There are a few things that are poisonous to dogs, like onions. But feeding your animals on your own goes back to the issue of trusting your own instincts and knowledge versus trusting the quality of the ingredients the pet food industry is using. I'll put my money on the pet owner any day.

Though it's beyond this book to provide pet food recipes, I've provided resources (see page 229) for learning more about various pet diets. At my house, I cook a weekly batch of quinoa, chicken, and vegetables for the dog that I alternate with raw chicken necks (never cooked chicken bones). I supplement with a multivitamin and my dog is healthy, has boundless energy, has no skin problems, and rarely needs to visit the vet.

CHAPTER ONE

CONDIMENTS, JAMS, SAUCES, AND SPREADS

THE RECIPES IN THIS CHAPTER serve as the foundation of your D.I.Y. kitchen. The mustards, vinegars, and sauces are combined with one another and other items elsewhere in the book to add flavor and versatility to your cooking, without additives or unnecessary packaging. Think of these as your own homemade "convenience foods." Time invested in making mustard, ketchup, vinegar, jam, or salsa is saved later when you utilize them to create simple and healthful meals. The first thing you'll notice is how easy it is to make most of these foods. The second thing you'll notice is how much better they taste than their supermarket counterparts—usually for much less money.

Customization is key. Learn how to make mustard from scratch, creating the flavor profiles you want. Your delicious, inexpensive, gourmet mustard can then be spread on sandwiches or whisked into homemade vinegar to make the best vinaigrette you've ever tasted. In minutes you can make a quick mustard glaze and use it to create a colorful and healthful side dish of roasted root vegetables or a simple and succulent pork roast. Perfectly spiced, fresh-tasting homemade ketchup easily becomes Texas-style barbecue sauce and can be incorporated into a homey stuffed cabbage recipe. Homemade jams appear in both sweet and savory preparations, and fresh nut butters can be used as is or made into desserts and sauces.

GRAINY PREPARED MUSTARD

Homemade mustard has so much more flavor than store-bought and has many uses in the kitchen. Whisk it with bourbon to make a glaze for pork (see page 36) or with maple syrup to caramelize root vegetables (see page 35), stir it into vinaigrette (see page 84), or simply spread it on sandwiches.

Mustard is simple to make, economical, and easy to vary to your taste. A word of warning: Your homemade mustard will always be quite a bit spicier than store-bought. You can control this somewhat by varying the ratio of brown to yellow mustard seeds (brown are more pungent). You can also add sugar, honey, maple syrup, or other sweeteners to temper the spice. You won't need to use much in a recipe or on a sandwich to get a big mustard flavor, and the mustard will mellow with time in the refrigerator.

Here is a basic formula with three variations, but I encourage you to create your own favorite recipe.

TIME REQUIRED: *about 10 minutes active; 24 hours passive*
YIELD: *makes 1 cup*

¾ cup liquid (mixture of vinegar and wine, beer, or some other alcohol; see Note, facing page)

½ cup mustard seeds (brown or yellow)

About 1 tablespoon finely chopped aromatics (onions, garlic, or shallots)

About 1 tablespoon chopped fresh herbs (optional)

About 1 tablespoon sweetener (sugar, honey, or maple syrup; optional)

Salt

Put the liquid, mustard seeds, aromatics, herbs (if using), and sweetener (if using) in a nonreactive (ceramic or pottery) bowl and let soak overnight in the refrigerator.

In a blender or food processor, blend the mustard to the desired consistency. Depending on your equipment and inclination, this can take up to 5 minutes. Don't expect your mustard to be as smooth as factory-made mustard. Season with salt as you blend. Transfer to jars and seal. The mustard will keep, refrigerated, for up to 3 months.

NOTE: *If you don't wish to use alcohol, replace the alcohol portion of the liquid with water. Mustards made solely with vinegar can be overwhelmingly vinegary.*

VARIATIONS:

BEER MUSTARD WITH THYME

½ cup hearty beer (not stout)

¼ cup champagne vinegar

¼ cup yellow mustard seeds

¼ cup brown mustard seeds

1 tablespoon finely chopped shallot

½ teaspoon chopped fresh thyme

Salt

Prepare as for basic recipe.

SHERRY-DILL MUSTARD

½ cup dry sherry

¼ cup sherry vinegar

¼ cup yellow mustard seeds

¼ cup brown mustard seeds

1 tablespoon finely chopped shallot

1 tablespoon chopped fresh dill

Salt

Prepare as for basic recipe.

HONEY MUSTARD

½ cup dry white wine

¼ cup rice vinegar

½ cup yellow mustard seeds

1 tablespoon finely chopped shallot

Pinch of allspice

1 tablespoon honey

Salt

Prepare as for basic recipe.

Maple and Mustard–Glazed Root Vegetables

This recipe provides a wonderful way to utilize your Grainy Prepared Mustard and makes it easy to turn humble root vegetables into an exciting side dish. Roasting the vegetables gives them a deep flavor and caramelizes their natural sugars. Since homemade mustard is quite spicy, it's nicely tempered by the sweet maple syrup. The green onions bring together the sweet, spicy, and savory with a touch of freshness and crunch.

TIME REQUIRED: *about 20 minutes active; 1 hour passive (excluding mustard preparation)*
YIELD: *4 to 6 servings*

3½ pounds mixed root vegetables (any combination of rutabagas, sweet potatoes, potatoes, carrots, beets, parsnips, celery root)

About 4 tablespoons olive oil

Salt

¼ cup maple syrup

2 tablespoons any version Grainy Prepared Mustard (page 32)

3 green onions, sliced on the diagonal (white and green parts)

Freshly ground black pepper

Preheat the oven to 400 degrees F.

Peel each vegetable and cut it into bite-sized chunks of roughly equal size. In a medium bowl, toss each type of vegetable separately in oil to coat and add a few pinches of salt. Lay each type of vegetable out in a single layer on parchment-lined baking sheets, keeping like vegetables with like vegetables, since they will cook at different rates.

Roast until the vegetables are soft, brown, and beginning to caramelize, 40 to 50 minutes, checking them every 10 minutes and removing the vegetables to a large bowl as each type finishes cooking.

In a small bowl, whisk together the maple syrup and mustard into a glaze.

When all the vegetables are cooked, pour the glaze over them and return them all to the baking sheets. Roast until the glaze thickens and the vegetables are warmed through, an additional 5 minutes. Transfer to a serving bowl, add most of the green onions, and toss. Season with salt and pepper, toss, garnish with the remaining green onions, and serve immediately.

Mustard and Bourbon–Glazed Pork Roast

Here is an uncomplicated, crowd-pleasing way to cook an inexpensive cut of meat. This recipe utilizes your Grainy Prepared Mustard and pairs well with a variety of side dishes. Leftovers can be used for Pulled Pork Canapés with Fig-Rosemary Jam (page 58), in sandwiches, on pizza, or stuffed into Corn Tortillas (page 128) with Simple Tomato Salsa (page 72).

TIME REQUIRED: *about 25 minutes active; 3 hours passive (excluding mustard preparation)*
YIELD: *6 to 8 servings*

One 4-pound boneless pork shoulder roast (ask your butcher to roll and tie it)

Salt

Freshly ground black pepper

½ cup lightly packed brown sugar

¼ cup bourbon

3 tablespoons any version Grainy Prepared Mustard (page 32)

Preheat the oven to 250 degrees F. Season the roast all over with salt and pepper.

In a heavy, dry cast-iron skillet over medium-high to high heat, brown the roast all over. Start with the fat side down, and turn with tongs until the roast is a deep caramel brown all over, 10 to 15 minutes. The fat from the roast should render, helping to brown the roast. (If the roast is very lean and you feel you need oil, use a tablespoon or so of refined vegetable oil suitable for high-heat cooking.)

Remove the roast to a plate and let the pan cool slightly. Pour off the excess fat and wipe out any burned bits. While the pan cools, in a small bowl, whisk together the sugar, bourbon, and mustard to make a glaze.

Return the roast to the pan and pour half of the glaze over it, turning the roast to coat it completely and using your hands to distribute the glaze evenly. Cover the pan with aluminum foil and roast for 2 hours, turning and basting every half hour with the remaining glaze.

Remove the foil and increase the oven temperature to 350 degrees F. Continue to roast uncovered, until the glaze reduces and the pork is glossy brown and thickly coated with glaze, 45 minutes to 1 hour. Let the roast rest for 10 minutes before slicing and serving.

REAL KETCHUP

I was pretty indifferent to ketchup until I learned to make my own. Commercial ketchup tastes mostly of sugar and is usually filled with stabilizers, additives, and high-fructose corn syrup. Real Ketchup tastes like tomatoes, with a nice balance of spice and a gentle sweetness. It's familiar enough that ketchup lovers will like it but refined enough to make a great barbecue sauce for Texas-Style Barbecued Brisket (page 39). When added to the sauce for Sarma: Serbian Stuffed Cabbage Rolls with Sauerkraut (page 188), it adds just the right touch of childhood familiarity. Real Ketchup takes a while to cook down, but this can be accomplished while you're in the kitchen (or nearby) doing other things. You just have to keep an eye on it and stir occasionally. Because it doesn't have the shelf life of commercial ketchup, it's best made in small batches.

TIME REQUIRED: *about 20 minutes active; 1½ to 2½ hours passive, but watchful*

YIELD: *about 1⅔ cups*

Two 28-ounce cans whole peeled plum tomatoes, or 3 pounds fresh Roma tomatoes, peeled and chopped (see Note, page 38)

½ medium yellow onion, cut into chunks

2 garlic cloves, peeled and left whole

½ cup cider vinegar

¼ cup sugar

One 2- to 3-inch stick cinnamon

2 teaspoons yellow mustard seeds

1 teaspoon cumin seeds

1 teaspoon whole cloves

½ teaspoon celery seeds

6 black peppercorns

½ teaspoon dry mustard

½ teaspoon cayenne pepper (or to your taste)

½ teaspoon salt

continued...

Put the tomatoes and their juices in a blender. Add the onion and garlic and blend until smooth. Pour the mixture through a fine strainer, pressing on the solids with the back of a spoon. Discard (or compost) the solids.

In a large pot over medium-low heat, bring the tomato mixture to a simmer. Lower the heat and cook, stirring occasionally, until the mixture is reduced by half and beginning to thicken, about 1 hour.

Meanwhile, in a small saucepan over medium heat, bring the vinegar, sugar, cinnamon, mustard seeds, cumin, cloves, celery seeds, peppercorns, dry mustard, cayenne, and salt to a boil. Stir to dissolve the sugar, turn off the heat, and let it sit while the tomatoes continue to reduce. When the tomatoes are reduced by half, strain the spice-infused vinegar into the tomatoes, discarding the spices. Continue to simmer the ketchup, stirring often, until thick, 20 to 30 minutes more. Taste for salt and spice, and adjust to your liking. Transfer to a jar and seal. The ketchup will keep, refrigerated, for 2 to 3 months.

NOTE: *If fresh tomatoes are used, the ketchup will take about 2 hours to reduce and thicken, will have a final yield of about 2 1/4 cups, and will be slightly less smooth than commercial ketchup.*

✓TIP: *The ketchup will taste sweeter, but less salty, when it is hot than it will after chilling, so use a light hand with the salt initially.*

Texas-Style Barbecued Brisket with Spicy Barbecue Sauce

Brisket is the traditional Texas barbecue-pit meat, but it can be a bit unpredictable and frustrating to cook unless you have a real smoker or pit. Buy a brisket with the fat cap left on and prepare to cook it low and slow for five or six hours, or you'll end up with great barbecue sauce on a piece of shoe leather. If you have a smoker, by all means do it the right way. For those with only a grill, I've devised this combination method. If you're intimidated, this recipe can easily be done with a friendlier cut of meat, such as tri-tip (and it won't take nearly as long). Or, you could do the entire recipe in a low, slow oven and skip the grill. You'll miss out on that smoky taste, but the smoked paprika makes a nice "cheater's 'cue." It's really about the tasty homemade barbecue sauce made with Real Ketchup anyway. Either way, start one day ahead as the meat needs to absorb the rub for at least 24 hours. Serve with cooked beans and Potato, Green Bean, and Radish Salad with Creamy Herb Dressing (page 82). It's also good with Corn Tortillas (page 128) or Flour Tortillas (page 136).

TIME REQUIRED: *30 to 45 minutes active; 30 hours passive (excluding ketchup preparation)*

YIELD: *8 to 10 servings*

SPICE RUB (MAKES ABOUT 1 CUP)

4 garlic cloves, peeled and left whole

Salt

¼ cup ground mild pure New Mexico chile powder

3 tablespoons lightly packed brown sugar

1 tablespoon dried Mexican oregano

2 teaspoons smoked paprika

1 teaspoon ground cumin

½ teaspoon cayenne pepper

½ teaspoon freshly ground black pepper

continued...

One 4- to 5-pound brisket,
fat cap on

Mesquite, alder, applewood,
or other wood chips

1 cup medium-bodied beer,
such as IPA

BARBECUE SAUCE (MAKES ABOUT
1 CUP)

¾ cup Real Ketchup (page 37)

½ cup apple cider vinegar

¼ cup lightly packed brown sugar

1 tablespoon soy sauce

1 teaspoon dry mustard

¼ teaspoon freshly ground
black pepper

To make the rub: Pound the garlic to a paste in a mortar and pestle with a pinch of salt.

In a small bowl, combine the garlic paste, chile powder, brown sugar, oregano, 2 teaspoons salt, paprika, cumin, cayenne, and black pepper. Mix to blend.

Reserving about 3 tablespoons of the rub for the mop, coat the brisket all over with the rub, using your hands to massage it into the meat so it penetrates into the grain. Wrap the meat well and refrigerate for at least 24 or up to 48 hours.

The morning of the day you plan to cook the meat, soak a couple handfuls of wood chips in water.

Start a fire in the grill for low indirect heat (keeping the coals over to one side of the grill). When the coals burn down to ash, and you can hold your hand over them for several seconds, or the grill temperature reads no higher than 250 degrees F, put the drained wood chips in a tin pie plate or sheet of aluminum foil, edges folded over but open at the top. Place the chip tin on top of the coals, but not covering them completely. Put the meat on the side of the grill away from the fire, fat-side up.

Make a mop by mixing together the beer and the reserved rub. Set aside for basting.

Cover the grill and cook the meat for 1 hour, basting with the mop, flipping, and rotating once halfway through. If you are using a real smoker, you can continue to cook until the brisket's internal temperature reaches 185 degrees F, another 3 to 4 hours, continuing to baste every half hour. If you're cooking on a grill rigged out as a smoker like I've described, baste the meat well, wrap it in foil, and transfer it to a 200-degree-F oven until the internal temperature reaches 185 degrees F, 3 to 4 hours. Unwrap and baste once and then re-cover and let rest before slicing.

To make the sauce while the meat rests: in a small saucepan, whisk together the ketchup, vinegar, sugar, soy sauce, mustard, and pepper. Bring to a simmer and cook, stirring occasionally, until thick and the flavors are blended, about 10 minutes.

Slice the meat very thinly against the grain and serve with the barbecue sauce on the side.

✓TIP: *You can mix up big batches of the Spice Rub and store it at room temperature in a glass jar, but leave out the garlic, adding it only when you are ready to use the rub.*

MEYER LEMON AND PARSLEY AIOLI

The word aioli *is often misused to describe any flavored* mayonnaise. *But it seems fitting to use the term* aioli *to indicate that this is special mayonnaise. Follow this basic recipe to make any variety of mayonnaise you like. Depending on how you are serving it, you might want to add cayenne, capers, anchovies, different types of herbs, or chopped, canned chipotle chiles. This is lovely in vegetable sandwiches, in BLTs, as a dip for roasted asparagus, or as a dressing base for potato salad. My very favorite use for Meyer Lemon and Parsley Aioli is to spread it on croutons and float them like buoys in Sustainable Seafood Stew (page 44). Of course you can make this in a food processor, but washing slippery mayonnaise out of a food processor always makes me cranky, while whisking it by hand is quick and soothing.*

TIME REQUIRED: *10 to 15 minutes active*
YIELD: *about ⅔ cup*

1 garlic clove, peeled and left whole

Salt

1 egg yolk, at room temperature

½ cup good, but not too pungent, olive oil

2 tablespoons freshly squeezed Meyer lemon juice, at room temperature

2 tablespoons finely chopped fresh flat-leaf parsley

Freshly ground black pepper

Pound the garlic to a paste in a mortar and pestle with a pinch of salt. Set aside.

In a medium bowl, whisk the egg yolk until smooth. Add the oil a few drops at a time, whisking continuously, and making sure that each addition of oil is incorporated fully before adding more. You can begin adding the oil more quickly about halfway through the process because the more oil the egg has incorporated, the less likely the aioli is to separate.

When all of the oil is incorporated, and the aioli becomes very thick and yellow, like lemon pudding, add the lemon juice a little at a time, whisking continuously. If you want your aioli to have a thinner consistency, add warm water a few drops at a time. Stir in the parsley and the garlic paste and season with salt and pepper. Transfer to a jar and seal. The aioli will keep, refrigerated, for 3 or 4 days.

To make in a food processor, follow the same procedure, adding the oil a little at a time through the feed tube while processing continuously.

Sustainable Seafood Stew with Meyer Lemon and Parsley Aioli Croutons

Seafood that's low on the food chain is healthier for both you and the oceans. Plus, it's tasty and economical. This recipe combines clams, mussels, and squid, but you could replace all or some of these with crab, lobster, or even sustainably caught or farmed fish, local to your area. You can gussy up this dish with chopped fresh tomatoes, citrus zest, or saffron, but it's quite good as is. A good trick for making a flavorful, quick stock is to ask the fishmonger for some heads or bones of fish trimmed that day. It's cheap, fresh, and flavorful. To shop for sustainable seafood, get a Seafood Watch card for your local area (see page 227) and take it to the store with you.

TIME REQUIRED: *about 1 hour active; 20 minutes passive (excluding aioli preparation)*
YIELD: *4 as a first-course or light-supper servings*

¼ cup olive oil, plus extra for croutons

½ medium onion, roughly chopped

1 celery rib, roughly chopped

1 medium carrot, roughly chopped

½ small fennel bulb, chopped

2 garlic cloves, left unpeeled and smashed with the side of a knife blade

Salt

1 pound fish heads and bones

½ cup dry white wine

3 or 4 sprigs fresh parsley

6 black peppercorns

Pinch of fennel seeds

½ baguette, sliced into ¼-inch slices on the diagonal

Freshly ground black pepper

1 pound mussels, washed and debearded

1 pound clams, washed

½ pound squid, cleaned (see Note, page 46)

Meyer Lemon and Parsley Aioli (page 43)

In a medium soup pot over medium heat, warm the ¼ cup oil. Add the onion, celery, carrot, fennel, garlic, and a few pinches of salt. Let the vegetables cook gently until soft and aromatic, about 10 minutes.

continued...

Add the fish heads and bones, 3½ cups water, the wine, parsley, peppercorns, and fennel seeds to the vegetables and bring to a boil. Skim any scum from the top and lower the heat to a simmer. Simmer until fragrant and the broth begins to color, about 20 minutes.

Preheat the oven to 400 degrees F. Lay the baguette slices on a baking sheet in a single layer, brush with olive oil, and bake until lightly toasted, about 7 minutes.

Remove the broth from the heat and strain it, reserving the fish for other uses (see "No-Waste Tip," below). Return the broth to the pot, taste, and adjust the salt, pepper, and acid by adding a little more white wine if desired.

Add the mussels and clams, cover, and simmer until they just open, 3 minutes or so. Add the squid and turn off the heat. Let sit, covered, for 30 seconds. Discard any unopened clams or mussels and ladle the stew into 4 warmed, shallow bowls. Spread the croutons with aioli and float in each bowl of soup.

NOTE: *To clean fresh squid, lay them all out on a cutting board near the sink. Position a bowl in the sink below the cutting board and have a colander ready in the sink. For each squid, pull the head free of the body and cut off the tentacles just above the eyes. Put the tentacles in the colander and pull out the remaining portion of the head with the eyes and guts that come with it. Discard them into the bowl with the ink sac. Using the dull edge of a knife, scrape the squid body so that the opaque, white viscera inside falls into the bowl. Do this several times to get out as much as possible. At the same time, scrape off the mottled skin so the squid is clean white. Turn the squid over and do the other side. Reach inside the body and pull the bony quill out, making sure to get it all.*

Place the cleaned squid in the colander with the tentacles and rinse thoroughly, letting the water run through the bodies to remove any remaining sliminess. Drain and cut the squid bodies into rings about ½ inch thick.

✓NO-WASTE TIP: *If you have a dog or cat, reserve the fish heads and trimmings after you strain your broth. Boil in fresh water until the bones are completely soft. Puree and add to your pet's food for a special, healthful treat.*

RED WINE VINEGAR

To make vinegar, you need four things: A vinegar mother (a mass of acetic acid bacteria); a glass, ceramic, or wooden crock of at least one-gallon capacity; two or more bottles of good red wine; and time—anywhere from three weeks to four months, depending on your vinegar mother. It's really quite simple and requires little actual effort. The quality of vinegar you can make at home rivals expensive specialty store vinegars. Most commercial vinegars are manipulated to hasten the conversion, and diluted. There is no substitute for time, though. Once you've tried your own vinegar, you will never want to use supermarket vinegar again.

These instructions and the mother I use are from Ken Cribari, of the original Cribari wine family (see page 49). Depending on where you obtain your mother, your instructions may be different and require different timing. Ask the person or business where you source your mother and experiment, tasting your vinegar often. See Sources on page 227 for supply information.

I use an Italian-made glass demijohn set in a straw-lined basket. These are much less pricey than the more common wooden barrels. I like them better because they allow easy access to the vinegar and don't have a spigot that can become clogged with mother over time. The straw-lined basket allows air to circulate, which is important. You can accomplish the same thing by setting a plain ceramic or glass vessel on top of a milk crate or a few bricks. A wide-mouthed crock is essential because the more surface area you have, the faster the conversion.

TIME REQUIRED: *about 10 minutes active; 2 to 4 months passive*
YIELD: *varies, depending on evaporation*

Two 750-milliliter bottles red wine (see Tip, page 48)   1½ to 2 cups vinegar mother

Using hot, soapy water, wash the crock (if it's wood, follow curing instructions) and a bowl large enough to hold the wine. Rinse well. Pour the wine into the bowl to allow the sulfites to dissipate. Let sit for 20 minutes.

continued...

Transfer the wine to the crock and add the mother and half of a 750-milliliter bottle of cool water. Swirl to aerate. Cover the crock with a towel or paper towel fastened with a rubber band. The vinegar needs to breathe, but you want to keep bugs out. Cheesecloth isn't the best because tiny fruit flies can get through it.

Store in a cool, dark place. The cooler it is, the longer the conversion takes. I was told my mother must not be stored anywhere hotter than 85 degrees F. But all mothers are different. Ask the person who gave you your mother.

Swirl once a month, tasting every 2 weeks. After the wine has turned to a vinegar you like (in 2 to 4 months), you can add more wine and water to fill the crock and let it continue to convert for another 2 to 4 months, or decant it, depending on the size of your crock. You can even add leftover wine now and again a little at a time, but this will slow things down.

When you want to extract vinegar, you can decant half the vinegar in the crock, leaving the mother behind, and replace it with an equal amount of wine diluted with water in the proportion above (1 part water to 4 parts wine). Or, you can empty your crock and start from scratch, removing the mother and giving some to other happy vinegar makers, while reserving some for your next batch. It will take much longer to produce a batch of vinegar starting from scratch each time. However, you will eventually have to clean out the crock and start over, as the mother will continue to grow and take over the crock. As this happens, parts of the mother will sink to the bottom and die. You can tell because the mother will look old and leathery and dark red. Take the dead mother out and compost it. The new baby will float in the vinegar. You don't need a lot of mother, so be sure to give some away when you decant.

✓TIP: *For choosing wine to make vinegar, the better the wine, the better the vinegar. Choose a good-tasting wine that you would drink yourself. You don't have to spend a lot, but you should never make vinegar with wine you wouldn't enjoy drinking. Don't add a wine if it is "corked" and don't add fortified wine such as sherry or Madeira to the vinegar crock.*

RED WINE VINEGAR
AND THE CRIBARI FAMILY

The Cribaris have been a respected wine-producing family since before Prohibition. Though they sold the main label many years ago, sacramental wine is still produced in California's Central Valley under the Cribari name. The Cribaris and my brother-in-law's family became close friends nearly fifty years ago, when both families lived in Lodi, California. One time, after visiting his friend Ed Cribari, my brother-in-law brought home a bottle of the most incredible homemade red wine vinegar I'd ever tasted. I never forgot it.

I'd tasted vinegar like the Cribari's once or twice, at specialty stores or food shows where good vinegar was being sampled. Vinegar of that quality is so expensive I never would have purchased a bottle. This homemade vinegar was so good, I had to learn how to make my own. So I arranged a trip to Ed and his wife Vickie's house to meet Ed's father, Ken, and to get my own vinegar mother, and the instructions to make vinegar.

Ken Cribari carries on the family's long-standing vinegar-making tradition from his home in Las Vegas, nurturing the vinegar mother his grandfather made over one hundred years ago. Ken makes his vinegar as a hobby, giving it away to family and friends. Each recipient receives a page of written instructions, and a little bit of mother just in case they would like to make their own vinegar.

The mother originated with Beniamino Cribari, who came over from Calabria, Italy, as a young man. He bought a small vineyard in Paradise Valley, California, and began pressing, fermenting, and selling wine locally. It was about that time that he started making vinegar.

Beniamino developed the mother himself from scratch. He made his vinegar in a ten-gallon wooden barrel and gave it to friends, much like Ken does today. When Beniamino died, Ken's uncle Tony, the youngest of Beniamino's four boys, took over the vinegar cask, which was then passed onto Ken, who carries the tradition on today, along with his son Ed. I'm proud to be part of the Cribari vinegar tradition, even though I'm not part of the family.

PLUM-VERBENA JAM

The combination of tart plums and fragrant lemon verbena is just so right. Easy to grow, lemon verbena is a perennial shrub with pointed, pale green leaves. It is sometimes available in high-end grocery stores. If you can't find it, it's okay to leave it out of the recipe, or experiment with other aromatic herbs like laven-der. If you do grow it, and have a good crop, another great use is to pair it with mint and muddle it with sugar for cocktails or lemonade. This jam will taste different depending on the type of plum you use, but I've tried it with many and it's always good. My favorite summer breakfast is homemade Yogurt (page 98) with fresh melon and a spoonful of this jam stirred in. You may want to top it with a little Granola Your Way (page 175), but it's great on its own. This is also a wonderful jam to use for Aunt Mil's Jam-Filled Sugar Cookies (page 53).

TIME REQUIRED: *about 45 minutes active; about 1 hour passive*
YIELD: *about 32 ounces*

3 pounds ripe plums (14 to 18 medium)	EQUIPMENT NEEDED
2 cups sugar	Eight 4-ounce jars or four 8-ounce jars with rings and lids
1 tablespoon finely chopped fresh lemon verbena	A set of canning tongs (see Tip, page 52)
	A large stockpot with a tea towel or water-bath canner with a rack
	Tea sack or cheesecloth

Put a small plate or saucer in the freezer to chill. You will use this to test the jam for the proper consistency.

Cut the plums into quarters and then chop them into pieces of roughly ½ inch. Put them in a medium, heavy saucepan. Add the sugar and set aside while you prepare the jars and lids.

Put the jars and canning tongs in a large stockpot. Add water to cover. Slowly bring the water to a boil while you cook the jam. Once it boils, turn off the heat and let the jars sit in the hot water until you are ready to fill them. This step is necessary for sterilizing the jars. Do not touch the jars with your hands once you have sterilized them, but use sterilized tongs.

Put the lids in a small bowl and pour boiling water over them. Let them sit until you are ready to use them.

Put the saucepan with the plums and sugar on the stove. Bring the plums to a simmer over medium heat, stirring occasionally, until the sugar dissolves and the plums begin to release their juices. Lower the heat to a very slow simmer and cook, stirring occasionally, until the mixture begins to thicken, about 20 minutes. Put the lemon verbena in a tea sack or in a square of cheesecloth tied into a bundle and add it to the plums. Continue to cook until the jam becomes darker in color and begins to thicken noticeably, 20 to 25 minutes more. To test for the proper thickness (gel point), drop a small spoonful of jam onto the chilled plate. Check it after 30 seconds; it should move slightly when you tilt the plate, but not run. If it runs, you need to cook the jam longer. If it doesn't budge, your jam might be over-firm. This won't hurt the jam, but as it ages, it becomes drier, and you may need to heat it before using.

With the tongs, remove the hot jars from the water bath, saving the water for processing, and place them, right-side up, on a tea towel. Ladle the hot jam into the hot jars, discarding the lemon verbena. Leave $\frac{1}{4}$ inch of headspace. If you see air pockets on the sides of the jars, dip a knife in the boiling water to sterilize and run it along the insides of the jars to eliminate.

Carefully wipe the rims of the jars with a clean damp cloth or paper towel. Place the lids on top and fasten the rings. Now you must process the jam. If you're using a canner, simply bring the water you used to sterilize the jars to a boil. Place the jars in the rack that comes with the canner and lower them into the boiling water. Process for 5 minutes. If you don't own a canner, use the large stockpot you used to sterilize the jars. Place a folded tea towel on the bottom of the pot to cover it and bring the water back to a boil. Using tongs, carefully place the jars on top of the tea towel, right-side up so none of the jars touch the bottom of the pot. Process for 5 minutes. Depending on the size of your jars and stockpot, you may have to process in batches.

continued ...

Remove the jars from the boiling water bath and place them on a clean towel to cool on the counter. After several hours, push down gently on the tops of the lids. The lids shouldn't move, bounce, or make a popping sound. If they do, they aren't sealed adequately to prevent spoilage. Refrigerate any jars that failed to seal and consume them first. Properly sealed jars will keep at room temperature for up to 1 year as long as there is no mold or obvious signs of spoilage. You can remove the rings after the jars are sealed and reuse them. Never reuse the lids.

✓TIP: *Though you can make do without a proper canning pot, I do recommend purchasing the special canning tongs. They have a wide, nonstick surface that makes it easy to fish the jars out of the water bath safely.*

Aunt Mil's Jam-Filled Sugar Cookies

These were always my favorite cookies growing up, and they still are. My Aunt Mil fills them with her crabapple jam from the trees in her yard. The cookies are soft, a little chewy, and very buttery. Another thing that sets them apart is their wonderful buttermilk tang. I tend to save my Cultured Butter for table use, since it's special, but you could certainly use it here (unsalted). I definitely recommend using the buttermilk from your Cultured Butter in these cookies, if you can time it properly. This is the cookie dough I always use for cutout, decorated cookies during holidays but they do just as well when served with tea or coffee anytime.

TIME REQUIRED: *about 1½ hours active; 8 hours passive (excluding butter and jam preparation)*
YIELD: *about 1 dozen*

4 cups unbleached all-purpose flour

1½ cups sugar

1 teaspoon baking soda

½ teaspoon kosher salt

1½ cups cold unsalted butter, cut into ¼-inch cubes

½ cup buttermilk, from Cultured Butter (page 121) or store-bought

2 large eggs, slightly beaten

1 teaspoon vanilla extract

¼ to ⅓ cup Plum-Verbena Jam (page 50) or jam of your choice

In a large bowl, whisk together the flour, sugar, baking soda, and salt. Cut the butter into the dry ingredients with a pastry blender or two knives until the mixture resembles cornmeal.

In a small bowl, whisk together the buttermilk, eggs, and vanilla. Add to the bowl with the dry ingredients and mix with a wooden spoon until smooth.

Gather up the dough into two equal portions. It will be very sticky. Wrap each portion well and flatten into 2-inch-thick disks. Refrigerate for several hours or overnight.

continued...

Preheat the oven to 425 degrees F.

Working with one portion of dough at a time, roll out the dough to $\frac{1}{3}$ inch thick. The dough will be sticky, so you'll need to use plenty of flour to roll it out, but try to use no more than you absolutely need or you may end up with tough cookies. It's a delicate balancing act. It's important to work quickly and keep the dough as cold as possible.

Using a 2-inch round cookie or biscuit cutter, cut the dough into circles. Dollop about 1 teaspoon of jam in the center of half of the circles and top with the remaining dough circles. Using your fingers, press down gently around the edges of each cookie to seal, working quickly. If you have special cookie cutters with patterned cutout shapes, you can use these for the top layer of cookie. They produce a pretty little "window" of jam. You can reroll and cut the scraps from your first batch one time, but you should refrigerate the scraps for 10 to 15 minutes first if it's an especially warm day.

Bake the cookies on an ungreased baking sheet until firm, fragrant, and lightly browned on the bottom, rotating the sheet halfway through for even browning, 8 to 10 minutes.

Transfer the cookies to a cooling rack. Store uneaten cookies in an airtight container at room temperature for up to 1 week. These cookies age well. I think they always taste better 1 to 5 days after I've baked them.

FIG-ROSEMARY JAM

Rosemary might sound unusual for jam, but it adds an interesting complexity that goes well with musky figs and citrus. The jam is subtle enough to taste good with toast or crumpets, but adds a twist to savory preparations like Pulled Pork Canapés (page 58). This is a small batch because figs are so precious. If you have a windfall, this recipe can easily be doubled without adjustments. If you want to make more than double this amount though, it should be made in batches.

TIME REQUIRED: *45 minutes active; about 1 hour passive*
YIELD: *about 24 ounces*

1½ pounds fresh Black Mission figs

1 cup sugar

½ teaspoon chopped fresh rosemary

¼ teaspoon finely grated lemon zest (Meyer, if available)

2 tablespoons freshly squeezed lemon juice (Meyer, if available)

Salt

EQUIPMENT NEEDED

Six 4-ounce jars or three 8-ounce jars with rings and lids

A set of canning tongs (see Tip, page 52)

A large stockpot with a tea towel or water-bath canner with a rack

Tea sack or cheesecloth

Put a small plate or saucer in the freezer to chill. You will use this to test the jam for the proper consistency.

Stem the figs and cut into eighths and put them in a medium, heavy saucepan. Add the sugar and ¼ cup water. Set aside while you prepare the jars and lids.

Put the jars and canning tongs in a large stockpot. Add water to cover. Slowly bring the water to a boil while you cook the jam. Once it boils, turn off the heat and let the jars sit in the hot water until you are ready to fill them. This step is necessary for sterilizing the jars. Do not touch the jars with your hands once you have sterilized them, but use sterilized tongs.

continued...

Put the lids in a small bowl and pour boiling water over them. Let them sit until you are ready to use them.

Put the saucepan with the figs and sugar on the stove. Bring the figs to a simmer over medium heat, stirring occasionally, until the sugar dissolves and the figs begin to release their juices. Lower the heat to a very slow simmer and cook, stirring occasionally, until the mixture begins to thicken, about 20 minutes. Put the rosemary in a tea sack or in a square of cheesecloth tied into a bundle and add it to the figs. Continue to cook until the jam becomes darker in color and begins to thicken noticeably, 10 to 20 minutes more. To test for the proper thickness (gel point), drop a small spoonful of jam onto the chilled plate. Check it after 30 seconds; it should move slightly when you tilt the plate, but not run. If it runs, you need to cook the jam longer. If it doesn't budge, your jam might be over-firm. This won't hurt the jam, but as it ages, it becomes drier and you may need to heat it before using.

Once the jam is cooked, stir in the lemon zest and juice and add a pinch of salt.

With the tongs, remove the hot jars from the water bath, saving the water for processing, and place them, right-side up, on a tea towel. Ladle the hot jam into the hot jars, discarding the rosemary. Leave $\frac{1}{4}$ inch of headspace. If you see air pockets on the sides of the jars, dip a knife in the boiling water to sterilize and run it along the insides of the jars to eliminate.

Carefully wipe the rims of the jars with a clean damp cloth or paper towel. Place the lids on top and fasten the rings. Now you must process the jam. If you're using a canner, simply bring the water you used to sterilize the jars to a boil. Place the jars in the rack that comes with the canner and lower them into the boiling water. Process for 5 minutes. If you don't own a canner, use the large stockpot you used to sterilize the jars. Place a folded tea towel on the bottom of the pot to cover it and bring the water back to a boil. Using tongs, carefully place the jars on top of the tea towel, right-side up so none of the jars touch the bottom of the pot. Process for 5 minutes. Depending on the size of your jars and stock-pot, you may have to process in batches.

Remove the jars from the boiling water bath and place them on a clean towel to cool on the counter. After several hours, push down gently on the tops of the lids. The lids shouldn't move, bounce, or make a popping sound. If they do, they aren't sealed adequately to prevent spoilage. Refrigerate any jars that failed to seal and consume them first. Properly sealed jars will keep at room temperature for up to 1 year as long as there is no mold or obvious signs of spoilage. You can remove the rings after the jars are sealed and reuse them. Never reuse the lids.

WHAT'S THE DEAL WITH PROCESSING JAM?

You may have noticed that many older preserving books don't call for processing jam in a water bath, but just for filling the hot jars with hot jam and then cooling until the jars seal. To be honest, I don't always process my jams, and have never had any trouble. Since the USDA now recommends it as an extra measure of sterilization, I give processing instructions in the jam recipes here. Please note that I would never take this risk with anything but jam, due to its high sugar and acid content. I always refrigerate any jars that fail to seal, whether they were processed or not, and I always refrigerate after opening.

Pulled Pork Canapés with Fig-Rosemary Jam

Here's an elegant way to repurpose your leftover Mustard and Bourbon–Glazed Pork Roast and it is a fun thing to try with your Fig-Rosemary Jam. Of course, you can use any leftover pork or any other jam you have on hand to make this rather impressive and inexpensive cocktail hors d'oeuvre.

TIME REQUIRED: *10 to 15 minutes active (excluding bread, pork, and jam preparation)*
YIELD: *18 to 20 pieces*

About ⅔ baguette, or 5 or 6 slices Half-Wheat Sourdough Bread (page 145) or Sourdough Cornmeal–Pumpkin Seed Bread (page 156)

About ¼ cup olive oil

1 cup shredded leftover Mustard and Bourbon–Glazed Pork Roast (page 36)

About 3 ounces soft, creamy blue cheese, such as Maytag or a locally produced version, at room temperature

4 ounces Fig-Rosemary Jam (page 55) or jam of your choice

Preheat the oven to 400 degrees F.

Cut the baguette into ¼-inch slices or cut each slice of homemade bread with a 1-inch biscuit cutter, to make perfect rounds. Arrange the bread slices on a baking sheet in a single layer. Brush with oil. Bake until browned and slightly crisp, about 7 minutes. Let cool slightly.

Put the pork in a small skillet over medium heat. Add a little bit of leftover Mustard and Bourbon Glaze, if available. If not, add a little oil. Toss the pork around in the hot skillet to heat and crisp it slightly. Set aside.

Spread each toasted bread piece with blue cheese. Top with a few shreds of hot, crispy pork, distributing it evenly. Top each canapé with about ¾ teaspoon of jam. Serve immediately.

PERSIMMON-SPICE BUTTER

I like to serve this spiced butter on wheat or rye toast topped with thin slices of Gruyère. Fuyu persimmons are more widely available than the bitter-until-squishy-ripe Hachiyas. This recipe makes a great gift, so you may want to increase the recipe and process it to make it shelf stable. (Follow the chart in a recently published canning book [see Sources, page 229]).

TIME REQUIRED: *about 2 hours active*
YIELD: *about 1 ¾ cups*

2½ pounds Fuyu persimmons, peeled and cut into 1-inch chunks

½ vanilla bean

⅔ cup sugar

2 tablespoons maple syrup

Seeds from 1 green cardamom pod, crushed or ground finely

One 2- to 3-inch-long cinnamon stick

2 tablespoons white rum

Zest of 1 lime (about ½ teaspoon)

In a food processor, puree the persimmons until smooth. You will have about 3 cups of pulp. For a smoother texture, put the pulp through a potato ricer or food mill. If you don't own one of these implements, don't worry, as the pulp will break down as it cooks.

Put the persimmon pulp in a large, wide, heavy-bottomed pot. Enameled cast iron works well. The wider the pot, the shorter the cooking time. Also, the taller the better, as the pulp will splatter.

Slice the vanilla bean up one side lengthwise, open it up, and scrape the tiny seeds into the pot with the pulp. Add the vanilla bean hull to the pot. Add the sugar, maple syrup, cardamom, and cinnamon. Set the pot over medium-low heat and bring to a simmer, stirring to dissolve the sugar. Adjust the heat so the pulp is just barely bubbling and cook, stirring occasionally and checking often to avoid burning and sticking until the pulp thickens and begins to turn dark, about 1 hour.

Add the rum and cook for another 10 minutes. Add the lime zest and turn off the heat. Let cool, remove the cinnamon stick, transfer to a jar, and refrigerate. The butter will keep for up to 2 weeks.

Apple Galette with Persimmon-Spice Butter

Tart apples and sweet Persimmon-Spice Butter make a very nice pairing when tucked into a flaky crust. Choose apples with a nice balance of sweet and tart that hold their shape when baked. I usually ask the vendor I'm buying from which ones he or she prefers for baking and then I taste them to see if the flavor seems right. This is the kind of uncomplicated dessert anyone can make. If you're intimidated by piecrust, don't worry. The cornmeal makes a sturdy, easy-to-handle dough. The true secret to flaky, tender crust is to keep the ingredients as cold as possible, work quickly, and don't overmix the dough. Stop when the liquid and the dry ingredients just barely come together.

TIME REQUIRED: *20 minuted active; 2½ hours passive (excluding persimmon butter preparation)*
YIELD: *makes one 12-inch galette*

3 tablespoons Yogurt (page 98)

⅓ cup cold water

1 cup all-purpose flour

¼ cup cornmeal

1 teaspoon sugar, plus about 1 tablespoon for sprinkling on top

½ teaspoon salt

7 tablespoons chilled butter (or a mixture of butter and lard divided fairly evenly), cut into small pieces, plus additional butter (melted) for brushing on top

About ¾ cup Persimmon-Spice Butter (facing page)

3 large or 4 medium apples, peeled or unpeeled, sliced thinly

In a small cup, stir together the yogurt and the cold water and place it in the freezer while you mix the other ingredients.

In a large mixing bowl, with a whisk, combine the flour, cornmeal, the 1 teaspoon sugar, and the salt. Add the chilled butter and work it in quickly with a pastry blender, leaving some pieces of fat the size of small peas.

Sprinkle the yogurt mixture over the flour mixture gradually, mixing it in with a fork. Be careful not to overmix. The dough should be crumbly, but stick together when pinched. You may not use all of the yogurt mixture.

continued…

Gather the dough into a ball, wrap and refrigerate for 2 hours.

Preheat the oven to 400 degrees F.

On a lightly floured board, with a rolling pin, roll out the dough to a $\frac{1}{4}$-inch thickness. Fold the dough carefully into quarters, pick it up gently and transfer to a baking sheet. Unfold the dough so it sits centered on the baking sheet.

Using a rubber spatula, gently spread the persimmon butter thinly and evenly over the dough, leaving a $1\frac{1}{2}$- to 2-inch border along the edges.

Lay the apple slices on top of the persimmon butter, working in a spiral from the inside out, covering the persimmon butter, but leaving the same $1\frac{1}{2}$- to 2-inch border. Fold the edges of the dough inward to encase the fruit, and sprinkle the entire galette with the 1 tablespoon sugar.

Bake on the center rack of the oven until the crust is brown and flaky and the apples soft and fragrant, 20 to 25 minutes. Halfway through, rotate the pan and brush the apples and the crust with the melted butter. Give the galette a final brush of butter when you remove it from the oven.

Let cool slightly before cutting. Serve warm or at room temperature. Store any leftovers at room temperature, covered, for no more than 24 hours.

FOOD PROCESSOR NUT BUTTERS

It's easy to make your own nut butters in an ordinary food processor, and they provide several advantages over store-bought nut butters. You control the smoothness to your liking; you can choose to make raw or roasted butters; and you'll never again worry about sodium, trans fats, sugar, or other additives. I've found homemade nut butters to be half the price (or less) of commercial ones. Since no stabilizers or preservatives are used in homemade nut butters, I like to make small batches of just a cup or two. Keep your homemade nut butters in the refrigerator, as they are highly perishable. If you like your butters ultrasmooth, you need not add any oil to them at all, just salt to taste. Continuous grinding will bring out the oils in the nuts, making the butters perfectly spreadable at room temperature. If you like them chunky, stop while the butter still has texture and add one to two tablespoons of vegetable oil (peanut oil works nicely) to make the butter spreadable.

RAW ALMOND BUTTER

Great on toast or a crisp fall apple, this butter also makes wonderful cookies. Try Almond Butter Sandwich Cookies with Spiced Pear Filling (page 64). You could also toast the nuts in a 350-degree-F oven for 10 minutes if you prefer a roasted almond butter. Let cool before grinding.

TIME REQUIRED: *about 15 minutes active*
YIELD: *1 cup*

2 cups (about 10 ounces) unsalted, raw whole almonds

1 to 2 teaspoons vegetable oil (optional)

Salt (optional)

Put the almonds in the bowl of a food processor and process until the butter is the desired consistency, stopping occasionally to scrape down the sides of the bowl, 5 to 8 minutes. Add the oil (if needed) and season with salt (if necessary). Watch the butter closely. Over time, it will progress from chunks of chopped almonds to small, dry pieces of almond to a cohesive ball of creamy, spreadable softness. Transfer to a jar and seal. The butter will keep, refrigerated, for up to 8 weeks.

Almond Butter Sandwich Cookies with Spiced Pear Filling

Here you have almonds and pears, a classic dessert flavor combination repurposed into a cookie. Fragrant mashed pears are gently infused with sweet spices and sandwiched between thin, nutty, crispy-chewy cookies to make this common dessert combo into something both homey and elegant. On its own, this pear filling makes a wonderful companion to ice cream or a filling for the Fresh Cheese Crêpes on page 112. I like to bake these in the fall when pears are at their best. Off-season, you can experiment with other fillings (jam, chocolate, or applesauce) or simply make almond butter drop cookies—like peanut butter cookies, only more interesting. The dough is a little crumbly and a bit difficult to roll out, but if you work with your fingertips to keep it together as you roll, it won't be too laborious. You'll need a spatula to transfer the cut cookies from the rolling board to the cookie sheet.

TIME REQUIRED: *about 1½ hours active; about 1½ hours passive (excluding butters preparation)*
YIELD: *24 sandwich cookies*

COOKIES

⅓ cup unsalted Cultured Butter (page 121) or store-bought unsalted butter, softened

⅔ cup Raw Almond Butter (page 63)

½ cup granulated sugar, plus extra for sprinkling

½ cup lightly packed light brown sugar

1 large egg

1 tablespoon unsulfured molasses

1 teaspoon vanilla extract

1½ cups unbleached all-purpose flour

½ teaspoon baking soda

½ teaspoon kosher salt

¼ teaspoon baking powder

SPICED PEAR FILLING
(MAKES ABOUT 1 CUP)

3 d'Anjou or Bartlett pears, peeled, quartered, cored, and sliced thinly

⅓ cup granulated sugar

One 2-inch cinnamon stick

4 whole cloves

4 whole green cardamom pods

1 star anise pod

½ vanilla bean, split down the side

continued...

To make the cookies: In a large bowl, using a handheld mixer, beat together the cultured butter and almond butter until well combined and creamy. Add the $\frac{1}{2}$ cup granulated sugar and the brown sugar and continue to mix until fluffy. Add the egg, molasses, and vanilla and beat just until combined.

In a small bowl, whisk together the flour, baking soda, salt, and baking powder.

Add the dry ingredients to the wet ingredients and stir to blend. If the dough seems crumbly, add 2 to 3 tablespoons of water a little at a time to bring it together. Form the dough into two equal-sized disks; wrap and refrigerate for at least 1 hour, or overnight.

To make the filling: In a medium, heavy-bottomed saucepan over low heat, combine the pears, sugar, cinnamon, cloves, cardamom, star anise, vanilla bean, and 2 tablespoons water. Cook, stirring occasionally, until the mixture begins to brown and turns syrupy, about 1 hour. Remove from the heat, remove the spices, and mash the pears with a potato masher until they resemble chunky applesauce. Return the pan to the stove and continue to cook over medium-low heat until the mixture is soft and fairly smooth, with a thick texture, another 20 to 30 minutes. Set aside to cool.

Preheat the oven to 350 degrees F.

If you've refrigerated the dough for several hours or overnight, remove from the refrigerator 15 minutes prior to rolling. Leaving one portion of the dough refrigerated, roll out the other portion on a lightly floured board to $\frac{1}{4}$ inch thick. You may need to stop and gently push the edges of the dough toward the center with your fingertips. You will find the dough somewhat crumbly, rather than sticky. Using a 2-inch round biscuit or cookie cutter, cut out the cookies. Using a spatula, transfer them to an ungreased baking sheet as you work. Gather up the scraps and reroll. The third round of scraps will probably need to be refrigerated before rerolling. Repeat with the other portion of dough, baking the cookies in batches. Sprinkle half the cookies with a bit of granulated sugar just before baking. The sugared cookies will be the tops of the sandwiches. Bake the cookies until brown and fragrant, rotating the pans halfway through, 6 to 7 minutes. Let cool completely on the sheet, then transfer to a platter.

When all the cookies are baked and cooled, assemble the sandwiches by placing 2 teaspoons of pear filling atop the unsugared cookies. Top each with a sugared cookie and serve. You can also make the cookies and pear filling up to 1 day in advance and assemble just before serving. Unfilled cookies can be stored at room temperature in an airtight container for 3 to 4 days. Filled cookies should be kept covered and eaten the day they are made, or frozen for up to 2 weeks.

ROASTED PEANUT BUTTER

Create a mind-blowing peanut butter and jelly sandwich with the Plum-Verbena Jam (page 50) and the Sourdough Cornmeal–Pumpkin Seed Bread (page 156). Or make a Spicy Southeast Asian Peanut Sauce (facing page) with it.

TIME REQUIRED: *about 30 minutes active*

YIELD: *1 cup*

2 cups (about 10 ounces) unsalted, raw shelled peanuts

1 to 2 tablespoons vegetable oil (optional)

Salt (optional)

Preheat the oven to 350 degrees F. Spread the peanuts on a baking sheet in a single layer. Toast until light brown and fragrant, about 15 minutes. Let cool completely.

Transfer the peanuts to the bowl of a food processor and process until the butter is the desired consistency, stopping occasionally to scrape down the sides of the bowl, 4 to 5 minutes. Add the oil (if needed) and season with salt (if necessary). Watch the butter closely. Over time, it will progress from barely chopped peanuts to tiny, dry pieces of peanut to a cohesive ball of creamy, spreadable softness. Transfer to a jar and seal. The butter will keep, refrigerated, for up to 6 weeks.

Spicy Southeast Asian Peanut Sauce

Make this with your homemade Roasted Peanut Butter or any other peanut butter. It's good to have on hand to turn simple food into exciting quick meals. Wrap leftover meat and vegetables in lettuce and use this as a dipping sauce. Toss rice noodles in it or drizzle it over steamed vegetables. I like to serve this sauce with baked or grilled chicken dunked in a quick marinade of pounded garlic, fish sauce, lime juice, water, and lots of black pepper.

TIME REQUIRED: *about 10 minutes active (excluding peanut butter preparation)*
YIELD: *1 cup*

1 or 2 serrano chiles, seeded and minced

1 garlic clove, peeled and left whole

Salt

½ cup Roasted Peanut Butter (facing page)

2 tablespoons freshly squeezed lime juice (about 1 lime)

1 tablespoon fish sauce

1 tablespoon vegetable oil (peanut oil is a good choice)

2 teaspoons sugar

Cayenne pepper (optional)

¼ cup chopped unsalted peanuts

With a mortar and pestle, pound the chile(s) and garlic to a paste with a pinch of salt. Transfer to a small bowl. Add the peanut butter, lime juice, fish sauce, oil, sugar, and cayenne to taste. Whisk until smooth. Check for a sweet, salty, spicy balance. Adjust seasonings by adding more lime juice, sugar, or cayenne as desired. Stir in the peanuts and add about ⅓ cup water to reach the desired consistency. The sauce will keep, refrigerated, for about 2 weeks.

ALL-PURPOSE RED CHILI SAUCE

This sauce is a great staple to have around. It's so easy to make and is a huge improvement over canned or jarred enchilada sauces. I use it in the Pinto Bean and Sweet Potato Enchiladas (page 132), but there are plenty of other ways to make it work for you in the kitchen. Add it to Mexican-inspired soup broths, pots of beans, egg dishes, or Chilaquiles (page 134), or make up a tamale pie with cornmeal dough and leftover Mustard and Bourbon–Glazed Pork Roast (page 36), using this as the sauce. It freezes well, too.

TIME REQUIRED: *about 30 minutes active*
YIELD: *about 2 cups*

5 or 6 dried ancho and/or New Mexico chiles

2 tablespoons vegetable oil

½ yellow onion, diced

3 garlic cloves, finely chopped

Salt

½ teaspoon dried Mexican oregano, crumbled

With scissors, slit the chiles up the sides and remove the stems and seeds.

Bring a kettle of water to a boil. Heat a medium cast-iron skillet over medium-high heat. Open the chiles up flat and lay them down in the skillet in a single layer. You may need to work in batches. Toast them for about 30 seconds per side, holding them flat and turning with tongs, until fragrant. Don't let them smoke or they'll turn bitter. Transfer the chiles to a small bowl and pour the boiling water over them. Push down to submerge them. Soak until soft, at least 15 minutes.

In the same skillet, warm the oil over medium heat and add the onion, garlic, 2 pinches of salt, and the oregano. Cook, stirring, until soft and fragrant, about 10 minutes. Turn off the heat and leave undisturbed.

When the chiles are soft, transfer them to a blender and add the sautéed onion and garlic. Blend until smooth. Wipe the skillet to remove any onion or garlic pieces and pour the sauce from the blender into the skillet. Cook over low heat, stirring occasionally, until thick and smooth, 10 to 15 minutes. This will help tame the natural bitterness of the chiles and blend the flavors. Season with salt. Use immediately, or let the sauce cool. Transfer to a nonplastic container, cover, and refrigerate for up to 7 days, or freeze for up to 1 month.

AVOCADO-TOMATILLO SALSA

If I had to live out life on a desert island and could take only one food item, avocado would be it. I love the smooth creaminess it lends to this salsa. Tuck this into the Zucchini and Mushroom Quesadillas (page 139) or use it to make Chilaquiles (page 134). It's also wonderful as a sauce on grilled chicken or beef.

TIME REQUIRED: *about 30 minutes active*
YIELD: *makes about 2½ cups*

1 pound fresh tomatillos

¼ teaspoon cumin seeds

½ medium red onion, cut into ½-inch slices

2 or 3 serrano chiles, left whole

3 garlic cloves, unpeeled and left whole

1 medium avocado

3 green onions, chopped (green and white parts)

3 tablespoons chopped fresh cilantro

Juice of 1 lime (about 1 tablespoon)

Salt

Freshly ground black pepper

Bring a pot of water to a boil, peel the papery husks from the tomatillos, rinse, and drop the fruits into the pot. Boil until they are soft and turn dull green, about 10 minutes. Drain and set aside.

While waiting for the water to boil, toast the cumin seeds over medium heat in a dry skillet until brown and fragrant, 5 to 7 minutes. Remove from the pan, let cool, and finely grind them in a spice grinder or with a mortar and pestle.

In a medium, dry skillet over medium heat, toast the red onion, chiles, and garlic, turning occasionally, until browned, fragrant, and soft, about 10 minutes. Remove them to a plate as they finish cooking.

When the garlic is cool enough to handle, peel it. Remove the stems from the chiles and some, none, or all of the seeds, depending on how hot you want your salsa.

Transfer the tomatillos, garlic, chiles, toasted onion, cumin, and the flesh of the avocado to a blender or food processor. Process until smooth, pour into a serving bowl, and stir in the green onions, cilantro, and lime juice and season with salt and pepper. You can make this salsa several hours or up to 1 day ahead. Extra salsa will keep for 3 or 4 days, covered well and refrigerated, but will discolor slightly.

SIMPLE TOMATO SALSA

Here's a simple, smooth, all-purpose salsa that is great for both cooking and dipping chips into. Enjoy this with Zucchini and Mushroom Quesadillas (page 139) or use it to make Chilaquiles (page 134). It's easy to adjust the heat to your liking by adding additional dried chiles or more or less cayenne. The classic Mexican technique of roasting the salsa ingredients in a hot, dry pan gives this salsa its authentic, smoky flavor. A well-seasoned cast-iron pan is best for this job, unless you happen to own a traditional Mexican clay comal.

TIME REQUIRED: *about 40 minutes active*

YIELD: *about 2 cups*

1 dried New Mexico or ancho chile

¼ teaspoon ground cumin seeds

½ yellow or white onion, cut into ½-inch slices

3 garlic cloves, unpeeled and left whole

1 pound fresh whole Roma tomatoes

1 small handful fresh cilantro leaves

1 tablespoon freshly squeezed lime juice, or more to taste

Salt

Freshly ground black pepper

Cayenne pepper (optional)

Using scissors, slit the chile up the side and remove the stem and seeds.

Bring a small pan of water to a boil. Heat a large cast-iron skillet over medium-high heat. Open the chile up flat and lay it down in the skillet. Toast it about 30 seconds per side until fragrant, turning with tongs. Don't let it smoke, or it will turn bitter. Transfer the chile to a small bowl and pour the boiling water over it. Soak until soft, at least 15 minutes.

In the same skillet, dry-toast the cumin seeds over medium heat until brown and fragrant, 5 to 7 minutes. Remove from the pan, let cool, and finely grind in a spice grinder or using a mortar and pestle.

In the same dry skillet, over medium-high heat, toast the onion and garlic until soft and brown, turning occasionally with tongs, about 10 minutes. Remove each one to a plate as it finishes cooking. Peel the garlic when it is cool enough to handle.

Put half of the tomatoes in the skillet and roast, turning often with tongs, until charred on the outside and beginning to soften, about 10 minutes. While they roast, peel the remaining tomatoes with a sharp knife and set them aside.

When all of the vegetables are roasted, and the soaked chile is pliable, remove the chile from the water, reserving the water to thin the salsa if needed. Put the chile, onion, garlic, and both the roasted and fresh tomatoes in a blender or food processor. Add the cilantro, cumin, and 1 tablespoon lime juice. Blend until smooth. Season with salt, pepper, cayenne (if using), and more lime juice to taste. Add the chile-soaking liquid if you desire a thinner salsa. Refrigerate, well covered, for up to 10 days.

AJVAR

Ajvar is a wonderfully versatile eggplant spread for sandwiches and impromptu appetizers, and a handy cooking ingredient. It's often found in specialty stores and I have always loved it. For years I assumed it was Middle Eastern, but I recently found out it's Serbian. Since I'm Serbian on my mother's side, and many of the recipes in this book originated in the house where she grew up, I love ajvar even more. Still, its unmistakable Middle Eastern character has me convinced that it came to the Balkans with the Turks. I don't remember eating this as a child, so I'm happy to bring it back into the fold. See the tips for using ajvar on page 22.

TIME REQUIRED: *30 minutes active; 30 minutes passive*
YIELD: *about 2 cups*

1 globe eggplant, about 1 pound

2 red bell peppers

2 garlic cloves, peeled

Salt

2 tablespoons freshly squeezed lemon juice

½ teaspoon ground Aleppo pepper (see headnote on page 191) or paprika

¼ cup extra-virgin olive oil

Freshly ground black pepper

Preheat the oven to 400 degrees F.

Wash the eggplant and poke it with the tines of a fork in several places. If you have a gas burner, lay it right on top of the grate, turn the burner to high, and roast until blackened all over, turning often with tongs, about 15 minutes. Alternatively, you can do this step under the broiler in your oven, but it won't yield quite the same charred character. Transfer the eggplant to a parchment-lined baking sheet.

Roast the bell peppers the same way and transfer them to the sheet as well.

Put the charred peppers and eggplant in the oven and roast until completely soft, about 10 minutes for the peppers and 20 to 30 minutes for the eggplant. Remove the peppers to a bowl, and cover with a plate so they can steam. Leave the eggplant in the oven until it is very soft all the way to the center. Test it with a fork to be sure.

Once the peppers are cool enough to handle, peel them, and remove the seeds and stems. Transfer the flesh to a food processor. In a mortar and pestle, pound the garlic with a pinch of salt until you have a smooth paste. Add it to the food processor with the peppers and pulse until chunky smooth.

When the eggplant is cool enough to handle, scrape the flesh from the skin and remove as many of the seeds as it is easy to do, without worrying too much about removing all of them. Transfer the eggplant to the processor with the roasted peppers and garlic. Add the lemon juice and Aleppo pepper and pulse a few times. Add the oil slowly while pulsing. Season with salt and black pepper. Serve immediately or refrigerate, well covered, for up to 10 days.

CHAPTER TWO

SALADS, DRESSINGS, BASIC APPETIZERS, AND MEALS

IF CHAPTER ONE IS THE FOUNDATION of your homemade kitchen, Chapter Two serves as the bricks you'll use to build it. We'll explore the numerous ways to combine the items in this book to make simple and quick meals from what you have on hand. Learn four basic salad dressings and what kinds of salads they complement best. Look for tips on varying the dressings for different dishes, or turning them into marinades or sauces that move effortlessly from the snack table to the dinner table.

The Great Salad Toss-Up Guide is a fun, mix-and-match method for choosing the proper main ingredients, dressings, seasonal vegetables, and embellishments to create stellar salads that are both healthful and satisfying.

SOY-GINGER DRESSING

Try this dressing on everything from green salads to Soba Noodles with Canned Wild Salmon (facing page) to brown rice salad to grilled fish. I like to keep it around to drizzle over steamed vegetables for a super-quick lunch.

TIME REQUIRED: *10 minutes active*
YIELD: *about ⅔ cup*

6 tablespoons unseasoned rice vinegar

2 tablespoons finely chopped peeled fresh ginger

1 tablespoon plus 2 teaspoons soy sauce

2 garlic cloves, finely chopped

1 teaspoon toasted sesame oil

¼ cup vegetable oil (such as peanut or sunflower)

In a small bowl, whisk together the vinegar, ginger, soy sauce, garlic, and sesame oil. Pour in the vegetable oil gradually while whisking continuously, until the dressing comes together. Transfer to a jar and cover. The dressing will keep, refrigerated, for up to 2 weeks.

Soba Noodles with Canned Wild Salmon and Soy-Ginger Dressing

Need a balanced dinner in less than twenty minutes? Here's a streamlined salad that makes a great pantry meal when you're feeling rushed. I always keep a few cans of wild Alaskan salmon in the cupboard for just such occasions. It's an affordable, sustainable seafood choice. Nori is the dried seaweed used in sushi rolls. It's readily available in many grocery stores and keeps well in the pantry. It has a savory flavor that adds a lot of character to a simple dish like this. The vegetable component can be varied according to the season and your inclination.

TIME REQUIRED: *20 minutes or less active (excluding dressing preparation)*
YIELD: *2 light-meal servings*

6 ounces dry soba noodles

8 asparagus spears, or 1 head baby bok choy

1 sheet nori seaweed

One 7.5-ounce can wild salmon, skin and bones removed, flaked

⅓ cup Soy-Ginger Dressing (facing page)

1 green onion, sliced on the diagonal (green and white parts)

2 teaspoons toasted sesame seeds

In a medium saucepan, bring a pot of salted water to a boil. Add the noodles and cook until tender, according to package instructions.

Meanwhile, if using asparagus, hold one end of each asparagus spear in either hand and snap each spear at its natural breaking point, discarding the tough bottom section of each spear. Cut the remaining parts of the spears into 1-inch pieces. If using bok choy, separate the leaves from the core and wash and slice the leaves into ribbons.

During the last 2 minutes of the noodle cooking time, add the asparagus or bok choy directly to the boiling water and cook along with the noodles. Drain the noodles and vegetables, rinse quickly with cool water, and set aside to drain well in the colander.

continued...

Turn one burner of a gas or electric stove to medium. Using tongs, hold the nori sheet over the burner and toast it until crisp and fragrant, moving frequently to avoid burning, about 2 seconds per section on both sides. Do not let it smoke. Set aside.

Transfer the cooled and drained noodles and vegetables to a bowl (pat dry if they still have water clinging to them) and add the salmon. Pour the dressing over and toss well. Using kitchen shears, cut the nori sheet into strips directly over the noodle salad, reserving a little for garnish. Add the green onion and toss. Divide the salad evenly between 2 bowls and garnish with the sesame seeds and the reserved nori. Serve immediately.

CREAMY HERB DRESSING

Here's a dressing that's super-easy to whip up at a moment's notice and is won-derful on a variety of different salads, such as Potato, Green Bean, and Radish Salad (page 82); just about any pasta salad; freshly steamed vegetables like spring peas and asparagus; or a green romaine salad. It also makes a very nice marinade for chicken or fish. If the dressing is too tart for your taste, add a tiny bit of honey to balance it. If you want something more like a classic green goddess dressing, increase the herbs and add minced anchovies and garlic.

TIME REQUIRED: *10 minutes active*
(excluding yogurt, crème fraîche, and mustard preparation)
YIELD: *1½ cups*

1½ cups Yogurt (page 98) or Crème Fraîche (page 116)

¼ cup chopped fresh flat-leaf parsley

1 tablespoon Honey Mustard (page 33)

1 tablespoon chopped fresh mint

1 tablespoon chopped fresh chervil or dill

1 teaspoon chopped fresh lemon thyme or regular thyme

½ teaspoon honey (optional)

Salt

Freshly ground black pepper

Whisk together the yogurt, parsley, mustard, mint, chervil, thyme, and honey (if using). Season with salt and pepper. Transfer to a jar and cover. The dressing will keep, refrigerated, for about 1 week.

Potato, Green Bean, and Radish Salad with Creamy Herb Dressing

Creamy Herb Dressing makes a wonderfully fresh dressing for this or any potato salad. Vary the vegetables according to the season. Spring's asparagus can stand in for summer's green beans. Cherry tomatoes and cucumbers also make nice additions. Steaming the potatoes whole makes for a better potato salad. It's super-easy, very fast, and it cooks the potatoes evenly without making them waterlogged.

TIME REQUIRED: *about 30 minutes active (excluding dressing preparation)*
YIELD: *6 servings*

1½ pounds small new potatoes (fingerlings or Yukon golds work wonderfully)

½ pound green beans, stemmed

1 bunch radishes, halved and thinly sliced (about 1 cup)

About 1 cup Creamy Herb Dressing (page 81)

Salt

Freshly ground black pepper

Scrub the potatoes and put them whole and unpeeled in a steamer basket. Steam over boiling water until tender, about 15 minutes (depending on their size). Test for doneness by inserting a paring knife into them. Remove and let the potatoes cool, reserving the water.

Add more water to the steamer if necessary and add the green beans. Steam until crisp-tender and bright green, 2 to 3 minutes. Rinse with cold water, then plunge them into a small bowl of ice water to stop the cooking.

When the potatoes are cool, cut them into bite-sized pieces and transfer to a large bowl. Drain the green beans and pat dry, and then cut them into 1½-inch lengths. Add them to the bowl with the potatoes. Add the radishes and the dressing. Toss until the vegetables are evenly coated. Season with salt and pepper and serve immediately.

This salad is best served right away because the moisture from the vegetables can cause the dressing to become watery. If you want to make it ahead, assemble the components separately, refrigerate them, and add the dressing at the last moment.

✓NO-WASTE TIP: *Not only does steaming potatoes make a better potato salad, but it's a smart way to save water and energy. Steaming requires less water than boiling and allows you to reuse the same water to steam the green beans and other vegetables. Also, your stove requires less energy to heat a small amount of water than it does to heat a large pot.*

BASIC BEST-EVER VINAIGRETTE

Everyone needs a simple dressing to have on hand for everyday green salads, potato salads, pasta, and beans. Why buy it at the grocery store when it's so easy to make? I've named this "best ever" because when it's made with your own Red Wine Vinegar and Grainy Prepared Mustard, it is. And the Tomato-Garlic variation (on facing page) is particularly good on bean and grain salads. Use the best olive oil you can afford and buy local or domestic if you can. If you find an imported extra-virgin olive oil that seems too cheap, it probably is. Counterfeiting is common in the global olive oil industry. What you think is pure olive oil may actually contain soybean oils or other cheap oils. See Sources (page 226) for domestic producers.

TIME REQUIRED: *10 minutes active*
(excluding vinegar and mustard preparation)
YIELD: *about ¾ cup*

3 tablespoons Red Wine Vinegar (page 47) or freshly squeezed lemon juice (for a lighter salad)

1 tablespoon minced shallot

1 teaspoon any variation Grainy Prepared Mustard (page 32)

½ cup extra-virgin olive oil

Salt

Freshly ground black pepper

Whisk together the vinegar, shallot, and mustard. Slowly drizzle in the oil, while whisking continuously, until the dressing comes together. Season with salt and pepper. Store in a covered jar refrigerated for up to 2 weeks.

TOMATO-GARLIC VINAIGRETTE

Add tomatoes and garlic to the Basic Best-Ever Vinaigrette and you've got a versatile dressing for bean, grain, or pasta salads, or for marinating or drizzling over cooked fish or chicken.

**IN ADDITION TO THE BASIC
VINAIGRETTE INGREDIENTS:**

1 garlic clove, peeled and
left whole

Salt

2 fresh Roma tomatoes, peeled,
or 2 canned Roma tomatoes

In a mortar and pestle, pound the garlic to a paste along with a pinch of salt. Add the tomatoes and pound them until smooth. Add to the finished basic vinaigrette.

Cannellini Bean Salad with Tomato-Garlic Vinaigrette

This is just one example of the versatility that can be achieved by combining cooked dried beans with seasonal vegetables and a great homemade vinaigrette. A freshly made warm bean salad can serve as an economical and substantial meal when paired with a grain, or bread and cheese. As a side dish, beans go well with grilled or roasted meats like Texas-Style Barbecued Brisket (page 39) and they're great to take to a potluck. This salad is best in winter, when radicchio is at its peak. In spring, you might include baby artichokes or asparagus; summer might call for cherry tomatoes and green beans; fall may bring roasted red peppers and eggplant from the garden. The Tomato-Garlic Vinaigrette goes well with any of the above combinations. Make sure you drain the beans thoroughly to prevent your salad from tasting watery.

TIME REQUIRED: *about 15 minutes active; 6 hours passive to soak and cook beans, (excluding dressing preparation)*
YIELD: *6 to 8 servings*

4 cups cooked and drained cannellini beans (see facing page)	½ cup chopped fresh flat-leaf parsley
2 celery ribs, cut in half lengthwise and sliced thinly on the diagonal	1 teaspoon chopped fresh marjoram
½ small head radicchio, cut in half, cored, and sliced thinly	½ teaspoon chopped fresh rosemary
½ red onion, sliced thinly	½ to ¾ cup Tomato-Garlic Vinaigrette (page 85)
About 12 pitted green olives (1 ounce), quartered	Salt
	Freshly ground black pepper

In a large bowl, combine the beans, celery, radicchio, onion, olives, parsley, marjoram, and rosemary. Add the vinaigrette (starting with ½ cup), and toss well. Season with salt and pepper, adding a little more vinaigrette if desired. Serve at room temperature within 3 hours, or cover and refrigerate for up to 5 days. Bring to room temperature and taste for salt before serving salad that has been refrigerated.

BEAN COOKING METHOD THAT YIELDS MAXIMUM FLAVOR

Leftover beans are great to have around for quick meals and snacks. They can be added to soups; tucked into quesadillas or tacos; eaten with eggs for breakfast or a light meal; pureed in the food processor with garlic, herbs, and olive oil to make a spread or dip; or tossed into a green salad with vegetables for a fast, nutritious meal.

YIELD: *about 6 cups beans*

1 pound dried beans, picked through for stones and rinsed thoroughly (see Tip, below)

3 tablespoons olive oil

1 small onion, chopped

1 celery rib, chopped (optional)

2 to 3 garlic cloves, chopped

Salt

Soak the beans in cold water to cover for at least 4 hours or overnight, if time allows.

Heat the oil in a large pot and add the onion, celery (if using), and garlic. Sauté until the vegetables are soft, about 10 minutes. Add the beans and their soaking water to the pot, unless the water looks dirty, then drain, rinse, and start with fresh water. Add water as needed to cover the beans by 1 inch. Bring to a boil and boil for 5 minutes. Lower the heat to a bare simmer, cover partially, and cook until the beans are tender, but hold their shape, 45 minutes to $3\frac{1}{2}$ hours (depending on the size and age of the beans), stirring occasionally. You may need to add water to keep the beans submerged.

Season with salt when the beans are nearly soft. Do not add tomatoes or any other type of acidic ingredient until the beans are nearly done, because acid inhibits their cooking. Remove from the heat and let the beans cool in their liquid. Cover and refrigerate for up to 5 days.

✓TIP: *Because dried beans that have been harvested within a year cook more evenly and have superior texture and flavor, choose beans from the bulk bins of a busy store or buy from a grower at your farmers' market.*

SIMPLE SESAME TAHINI DRESSING

Besides being tasty on grain and Asian noodle salads, this dressing is also fantastic drizzled over grilled fish or chicken or fresh sliced tomatoes, or used as a sandwich spread. Tahini is a paste made from ground sesame seeds, used often in Middle Eastern cuisine (it's one of the essential ingredients in hummus). You can find tahini in both raw and roasted versions, in either jars or cans. It is produced both domestically and overseas. Look for it in health food and specialty stores and in the world foods aisle in some grocery stores. Any type of tahini can be used in this recipe. I buy locally produced organic, raw tahini from Artisana. Tahini should be refrigerated after opening as it goes rancid quickly.

TIME REQUIRED: *about 10 minutes active*
YIELD: *about ³/₄ cup*

2 garlic cloves, peeled and left whole

Salt

¹/₃ cup sesame tahini paste

3 tablespoons freshly squeezed lemon juice

2 teaspoons honey

1 teaspoon soy sauce

¹/₄ teaspoon toasted sesame oil

With a mortar and pestle, pound the garlic to a paste with a pinch of salt. In a blender, combine the garlic paste, tahini, ¹/₃ cup water, the lemon juice, honey, soy sauce, and sesame oil and blend until smooth. Season with salt. Use immediately or cover and refrigerate for up to 2 weeks.

Wheat Berry Salad with Roasted Beets, Kale, Toasted Walnuts, and Simple Sesame Tahini Dressing

This is just one of many different seasonal grain salads that can be made with the Simple Sesame Tahini Dressing. You can vary the grain by using brown or other types of rice, farro, quinoa, or kamut. Likewise, vary the vegetables seasonally. In summer, you'll want to use tomatoes, green beans, and cucumbers; in fall, roasted squash and pumpkin seeds; in spring, sweet peas, asparagus, or fava beans. You could also add shredded leftover chicken, canned wild salmon, or hard-cooked eggs for protein.

TIME REQUIRED: *about 45 minutes active; 1 hour passive*
YIELD: *6 servings*

4 small to medium beets (see Tip, page 91)

½ cup (about 2 ounces) walnut halves, coarsely chopped

1 cup wheat berries, soaked for 4 to 5 hours or overnight and drained

Salt

1 bunch Lacinato or green or red kale

¾ cup Simple Sesame Tahini Dressing (facing page)

Freshly ground black pepper

Preheat the oven to 400 degrees F.

Trim the beets and wrap them in one or two foil packets, depending on their size, keeping like-sized beets with like-sized beets. Put them in a baking dish to prevent beet juice from leaking into your oven and roast until tender and fragrant, 35 to 40 minutes. Use a small paring knife or skewer to check for doneness. The knife or skewer should go in easily with a small amount of resistance. Set them aside to steam in their foil packets. When they are cool enough to handle, peel them by rubbing the skins off with your fingertips, and then cut the beets into bite-sized wedges. Alternatively, the beets can be roasted up to 5 days ahead and refrigerated, left in their foil wrappers, until ready to use.

Lower the oven temperature to 300 degrees F.

In a small baking dish, arrange the walnuts in a single layer. Toast until brown and fragrant, 8 to 10 minutes. Remove from the oven and let cool.

continued...

While the beets are roasting and the walnuts are toasting, set a medium sauce-pan with 3 cups of water over medium-high heat. Bring to a boil and add the wheat berries and a pinch of salt. Lower the heat to a slow simmer, cover partially, and cook until tender and pleasantly chewy, 45 to 50 minutes. Turn off the heat and let the wheat berries sit until you are ready to assemble the salad.

Meanwhile, trim, stem, and wash the kale and put it in a vegetable steamer set over boiling water. Steam until tender and wilted, but still bright green, about 5 minutes. Remove immediately to a bowl of ice water to stop the cooking. Drain and squeeze out excess moisture. Chop coarsely and set aside.

When all the ingredients are ready, drain the wheat berries and transfer them to a serving bowl. Add the beet wedges, kale, and walnuts. Add the dressing and toss thoroughly. Taste and correct the seasoning with salt and pepper and serve immediately or within 2 hours at room temperature. The salad can also be covered and refrigerated for 3 to 4 days. Bring to room temperature before serving.

✓TIP: *I like to roast beets this way whenever I have the oven on for something else. It's an energy-saving strategy and a great way to have cooked beets on hand for adding to salads anytime.*

The Great Salad Toss-Up Guide

Do you want to eat more seasonally, locally, sustainably, and healthfully, and avoid falling back on supermarket takeout or restaurants after a busy day? Here's a system to do that, but first you must banish the image of a typical green salad from your mind.

Shop your farmers' market and buy a variety of seasonal vegetables to have on hand. Keep your pantry stocked with grains and legumes. Cook one variety of grain and legume each over the weekend to have on hand for the week, and you'll be able to create flavorful, balanced salad meals very quickly.

Make extra and brown-bag your lunch. Think of meat as an occasional embellishment, use up leftover cooked vegetables from other meals, and you'll have a zero-waste, economical, and sustainable kitchen, and you'll get plenty of vegetables in your diet without even trying.

Look at the four salad recipes in this chapter, read the seasonal suggestions in their head notes, and consider the tips below to begin to get a feel for good combinations. Pretty soon you'll be creating your own favorites by instinct and by the season.

Use the lists on pages 94 and 95 to follow this four-step system for creating endless salads whatever the season or your mood.

1. Choose 1 salad base (or combine a grain and legume).

2. Add 2 or 3 vegetable and/or protein additions, depending on what's in season and what sounds good to you.

3. Add 1 or 2 garnishes and embellishments.

4. Choose your dressing, and toss.

Lentils, roasted beets, slivered fennel, arugula, feta, and Basic Best-Ever Vinaigrette (page 84) made with lemon juice

Brown rice, corn, cherry tomatoes, sautéed summer squash, Fresh Whole-Milk Soft Cheese (page 106), and Tomato-Garlic Vinaigrette (page 85)

Quinoa with sautéed mushrooms, mustard greens, sugar snap peas, Spicy Kimchi (page 191), sesame oil, and Soy-Ginger Dressing (page 78)

Potatoes with roasted asparagus, radishes, mixed fresh herbs, and Creamy Herb Dressing (page 81)

Chickpeas with roasted red peppers, green beans, avocado, olives, and Simple Sesame Tahini Dressing (page 88)

Rice noodles with shredded Mustard and Bourbon–Glazed Pork Roast (page 36), sugar snap peas, green onions, sesame oil, and Soy-Ginger Dressing (page 78)

Wheat berries, roasted butternut squash cubes, sautéed chard, toasted walnuts or pumpkin seeds, goat cheese, and Basic Best-Ever Vinaigrette (page 84)

THE PROBLEM WITH TUNA

You may have noticed that I recommend canned wild salmon, herring, and sardines, but not tuna. That's because many species of tuna are endangered and others are caught using methods that harm the environment. Also, larger, longer-lived species of tuna can have high levels of mercury. Since it's hard to know which type of tuna is in those little cans or how it was caught, I usually avoid it unless I can find hook-and-line caught (but not long-line caught) skipjack or some other small breed of tuna. Go to www.montereybayaquarium.org/cr/seafoodwatch.aspx to learn more about choosing sustainable seafood.

SALAD BASES

- Beans and legumes: any kind, from black beans to lentils to chickpeas
- Potatoes: new potatoes, fingerlings, small red potatoes, and sweet Yukon golds are fantastic for salads
- Grains: wheat berries, quinoa, brown rice, farro, kamut, barley
- Soba and rice noodles

VEGETABLE AND PROTEIN ADDITIONS

- Roasted beets
- Roasted red peppers
- Arugula, endive, or radicchio
- Steamed or roasted asparagus
- Sautéed or steamed chard, kale, mustard greens, or collards
- Sautéed mushrooms
- Steamed green beans, snow peas, or sugar snap peas
- Roasted cubed squash or sweet potatoes
- Tomatoes
- Cucumbers
- Corn, cut off the cob
- Thinly sliced fennel
- Sautéed summer squash
- Radishes
- Sea vegetables, such as wakame or hijiki
- Hard-cooked egg
- Canned fish: wild salmon, mackerel, or sardines
- Leftover shredded chicken, pork, or beef

GARNISHES AND EMBELLISHMENTS

- Simple Wild Sauerkraut (page 186)
- Spicy Kimchi (page 191)
- Micro greens or sprouts
- Gomashio (a flavorful mixture of sesame seeds, salt, and sometimes seaweed that is used in Japanese and macrobiotic cooking)
- Toasted nori
- Green onions
- Sesame oil
- Fresh Whole-Milk Soft Cheese (page 106), feta, blue cheese, or creamy goat cheese
- Fresh herbs: basil, chervil, savory, cilantro, and parsley
- Olives
- Avocado
- Toasted nuts and seeds

DRESSINGS

- Creamy Herb Dressing (page 81)
- Basic Best-Ever Vinaigrette (page 84) with lemon, vinegar, or Tomato-Garlic Vinaigrette (page 85)
- Simple Sesame Tahini Dressing (page 88)
- Soy-Ginger Dressing (page 78)

CHAPTER THREE

DAIRY PRODUCTS

THE DAIRY PRODUCTS YOU WILL FIND in this chapter start simply—with milk or cream and some sort of culturing or curdling agent. It's my intention to provide a useful repertoire of dairy products boiled down to a few simple formulas and techniques. If you are interested in learning more about making your own dairy products or getting into more complicated cheeses, there are resources (see page 226) in the back of this book to help you.

There is nothing more satisfying than watching your own fresh cheese form curds or tasting your own homemade tangy yogurt or creamy cultured butter for the first time. Many commercial dairy products are full of artificial flavors, stabilizers, and colors. Not so with homemade. And it's a simple process that anyone can master. All you need is good milk or cream and a few simple tools. The dairy products in this chapter can be made by anyone, in any home kitchen. The methods are simple and streamlined and avoid the use of special equipment whenever possible. You'll find four fresh and delicious homemade dairy products and a variety of special recipes that utilize them—everything from pasta to crêpes to a cake.

YOGURT

Plain, full-fat yogurt is a staple in my house. I eat it for breakfast with honey, fresh fruit, and Granola Your Way (page 175). It's also great with maple syrup or jam stirred in. Sometimes I drizzle it into whole-grain porridge (see page 179); drain it to transform it into thick, creamy dressings and dips; dollop it on Simple Dal (page 203) or spicy grilled chicken; blend it with fresh summer fruit into smoothies; or add it to baked goods for a luscious tang. It's very easy to make yogurt without a yogurt maker, but you will need a method for keeping your yogurt warm while it cultures. Read the FAQs on page 100 before getting started.

TIME REQUIRED: *20 minutes active; 20 minutes passive, but watchful; 8 to 10 hours passive*

YIELD: *1 quart*

1 quart of the best milk available (I use non-homogenized, full-fat organic cow's milk from a local dairy, but you can use low-fat milk if you prefer)

2 tablespoons plain yogurt with active cultures, or 1 teaspoon powdered yogurt starter

EQUIPMENT NEEDED

A candy or dairy thermometer (optional but helpful)

A one-quart mason jar

A whisk that will fit into the mason jar

Pour the milk into a large saucepan and turn the heat to medium-low. Heat it slowly, stirring occasionally, until it is just below the boiling point, about 20 minutes. Watch carefully and do not allow it to boil. If you have a thermometer, the milk should be about 185 degrees F. There are some visual and olfactory cues to look for if you don't have a thermometer. Tiny bubbles will form just under the skin that covers the surface of the milk. The surface will undulate slightly, but the bubbles shouldn't break the surface. The milk will have a cheesy, scalded aroma. Once the milk reaches this state, hold it there for 5 minutes.

While you wait for the milk to come up to temperature, sterilize a 1-quart mason jar and its lid with boiling water. Let them air-dry. Warm a large pot of water for a water bath, if using.

Once the milk has remained at 185 degrees F for 5 minutes, remove it from the heat and let it cool down to 115 degrees F, stirring occasionally. This will take 20 to 30 minutes.

Put the yogurt or starter in the bottom of the sterilized mason jar and add about $\frac{1}{2}$ cup of the cooled milk. Whisk to blend well. Add the remaining cooled milk, stirring well to distribute the cultures throughout. Fasten the lid and place the jar in your incubator of choice for 8 to 10 hours.

Remove the jar from the incubator and refrigerate it until cool before eating. If your yogurt is a little lumpy, simply whisk it smooth before eating. If you would like thicker yogurt, strain it to the desired thickness in a coffee filter set in a strainer over a bowl. The whey that drains off can be used to soak grains, cook beans, or ferment beets (see page 197).

EASY YOGURT CHEESE

Drain 1 quart of yogurt in the refrigerator in a coffee filter set over a strainer for 12 hours and you have yogurt cheese. It's sublime with fresh, sweet strawberries and makes an impressive appetizer with olive oil and the Middle Eastern spice za'atar. Serve it with Ajvar (page 74), assorted pickles (see pages 200 and 201), and Whole-Wheat Sesame Crackers (page 169). One quart of yogurt yields about $1\frac{1}{3}$ cups of yogurt cheese.

FREQUENTLY ASKED YOGURT QUESTIONS

WHY MAKE YOGURT?

1. If you find yourself drowning in plastic yogurt containers, making your own yogurt will solve that problem.

2. It may be difficult for you to find good-quality, plain yogurt without additives, gums, or thickeners.

3. Sometimes supermarket yogurt is super-heated, which kills some of the beneficial live cultures.

4. You'll save money because fresh, organic milk is less expensive than organic yogurt.

CAN I USE A YOGURT MAKER?

You can buy a yogurt maker if you want to be completely foolproof, but all you really need is yogurt starter, a thermometer, and a method for keeping your yogurt at a steady 90 to 100 degrees F for 8 to 10 hours.

WHAT KIND OF STARTER SHOULD I USE?

You can use plain store-bought active yogurt, and your own homemade yogurt after that, or powdered yogurt culture bought in a grocery or natural foods store. Powdered culture will give you more consistent results and is necessary if you forget to hold back some yogurt for the next batch.

Powdered starter is available in small jars in the refrigerated section where dietary supplements are sold. The directions on the jar will tell you how much to use. You can also purchase yogurt starter from a cheese supply house (see page 226).

WHAT'S THE BEST WAY TO INCUBATE YOGURT?

You may have to experiment a couple of times until you find the method that works best for you, but below are a few ideas.

1. Put a quart jar of ripening yogurt in a large pot of water heated to 90 to 100 degrees F and keep the whole thing in the oven overnight with the light on, or in a gas oven with the pilot light on.

2. Wrap the jar in a black plastic garbage bag and leave it in the sun on an 80- to 85-degree-F day for about 8 hours.

3. Put the yogurt in a warm water bath and set the whole thing in an insulated cooler with towels wrapped around it for 8 to 10 hours.

4. Wrap a heating pad set on low around a jar of ripening yogurt for 8 to 10 hours.

5. Make the yogurt directly in a pre-warmed insulated thermos and keep it in a warm place while it cultures.

Beet and Turnip Salad with Yogurt and Herbs

This salad is the essence of uncomplicated deliciousness. All you do is steam the vegetables, whisk herbs into the Yogurt (see Tip, below), and toss it together. Because the turnips will cook faster than the beets, steam the vegetables separately or use a two-level steamer that allows you to cook both at once, separately. Vary the herbs according to your taste and what's in your garden.

TIME REQUIRED: *10 minutes active; 25 minutes passive (excluding yogurt preparation)*
YIELD: *4 servings*

1 pound Tokyo (small white) or golden turnips, trimmed, or regular turnips, quartered

1 pound medium beets, trimmed

2/3 cup Yogurt (page 98)

1 tablespoon snipped fresh chives

1 tablespoon chopped fresh parsley

2 teaspoons chopped fresh dill

Pinch of fresh thyme

Salt

Freshly ground black pepper

Place the turnips and beets on separate levels of a two-level steamer. If you only have one level, start the beets first as they will take 5 to 10 minutes longer. Turn the heat to medium, bring to a boil, and steam until the vegetables are tender, checking the water level occasionally, and adding more if necessary. The turnips will take about 15 minutes and the beets about 25 minutes.

In a small bowl, whisk together the yogurt, chives, parsley, dill, and thyme (or whatever herbs you are using). Season with salt and pepper. Set aside.

Remove the vegetables from the heat, let cool, and peel the beets. Cut the beets and turnips into bite-sized wedges and transfer them to a medium bowl. Pour the herbed yogurt over, toss to coat, and season with salt and pepper. Serve immediately.

TIP: *The yogurt can be mixed with the herbs a couple of hours ahead of time, and the vegetables can be steamed and refrigerated up to 2 days ahead. It's best not to mix the vegetables and yogurt until you are ready to serve, as the beets stain the salad and the yogurt becomes watery. If you've cooked the vegetables ahead and refrigerated them, bring them to room temperature before tossing with the yogurt and serving.*

Stone Fruit–Yogurt Cake with Cornmeal and Walnut Streusel

This cake is perfect for nonbakers because it's easy and foolproof. Inspired by a bumper crop of plums from a relative's tree and my own homemade yogurt, I created this one summer day. The streusel was my friend Haven Bourque's suggestion. This has become my signature cake and may become yours as well. It's a great way to use frozen, sliced stone fruit of any sort, any time of year. Apples or pears, sautéed until soft before folding into the cake, are also a great idea.

TIME REQUIRED: *about 30 minutes active; 45 minutes passive (excluding butter and yogurt preparation)*
YIELD: *8 to 10 servings*

1½ cups unbleached all-purpose flour

½ cup yellow cornmeal

1½ teaspoons baking powder

½ teaspoon kosher salt

½ teaspoon baking soda

8 tablespoons Cultured Butter (page 121) or store-bought butter, softened

½ cup granulated sugar

½ cup lightly packed brown sugar

2 large eggs

1 teaspoon vanilla extract

⅔ cup plain whole-milk Yogurt (page 98)

3 cups sliced fresh or thawed frozen plums or other fruit

1 cup (about 4 ounces) pecan or walnut halves, lightly toasted and roughly chopped

Preheat the oven to 350 degrees F.

Lightly butter and flour a 10-inch round cake pan. You can use a springform pan if you want to unmold it and serve it on a platter.

In a small bowl, sift together the flour, cornmeal, baking powder, salt, and baking soda.

continued...

In a large bowl, using a handheld mixer, beat together the butter, granulated sugar, and ¼ cup of the brown sugar until creamy. Add the eggs and vanilla and mix to combine.

Add the dry ingredients and the yogurt to the sugar mixture in two additions, starting with the dry ingredients and ending with the yogurt. Fold in the fruit.

Pour the batter into the prepared pan. Mix together the nuts and the remaining brown sugar and sprinkle over the top of the cake.

Bake on the middle shelf of the oven, until the cake rises in the center and browns, and a toothpick inserted into the cake comes out clean, about 45 minutes. Set the cake on a cooling rack and let it cool completely before cutting and serving, or removing from the pan. Wrap any leftovers well and store at room temperature for up to 2 days. The cake will keep, refrigerated, for 1 week, or may be frozen for 1 month, if wrapped well, whole or in pieces.

FRESH WHOLE-MILK SOFT CHEESE

There is a whole class of cheese made using this method. Ricotta is one, though it was traditionally made from the whey left over from making hard cheeses. This recipe makes a cheese similar to whole-milk ricotta. The same process is used to make queso blanco and panir, but that soft Indian cheese is lightly pressed. Whatever you call this fresh cheese, it's versatile; is easy for anyone to make; and tastes clean, sweet, and milky. You can create your own particular style of fresh cheese by adjusting the time you drain the cheese and the thickness of your cheesecloth. You can even try cutting holes in a plastic or metal container to make a cheese mold and then fashioning a press to make a pressed cheese. When moist, this cheese is good for spreading and using as a dessert filling. Drain it longer, and it's perfect for pizza and pasta.

TIME REQUIRED: *10 minutes active; 1 hour mostly passive, yet watchful*
YIELD: *about 1¼ pounds, depending on how much whey you drain out*

1 gallon whole milk (not ultra-pasteurized as you may have trouble curdling it)

⅓ cup white or apple cider vinegar, or ½ cup freshly squeezed lemon juice

Non-iodized salt, such as kosher or cheese salt (optional; see Sources, page 226)

Pour the milk into a large nonreactive pot (stainless steel, ceramic, or enameled). Over medium-low heat, slowly bring up the milk temperature to 185 degrees F, stirring occasionally. Take your time, so you don't scorch the milk. Stir occasionally and watch closely. This can take 45 minutes or longer.

While you wait, ready two, four, or six layers of cheesecloth (the number of layers depends on how dry you want your cheese), folded into a square of about 18 inches on each side. Place the cheesecloth in a strainer. Fewer layers will make the cheese drain more quickly and yield a drier, crumblier cheese.

continued...

If you don't have an accurate thermometer, you can still make ricotta. The milk should be just short of boiling. Signs that the milk is almost ready include tiny bubbles on the sides of the pan and a shimmering, vibrating surface not yet broken by bubbles.

When the milk reaches the proper temperature, turn off the heat, pour in the vinegar and stir to distribute. Stop stirring and let the milk sit undisturbed for 5 to 8 minutes. You will see curds begin to form and separate from the whey. Using a slotted spoon or small, handheld strainer, spoon the curds out into the cheesecloth-lined strainer. It will look a little like wet biscuit dough. Work the cheese a little with a spoon to release some of the liquid. Tie the ends of the cheesecloth together so you have a bundle of cheese and hang it from a wooden spoon set across a big pot until it reaches the desired consistency (5 to 10 minutes). Reserve the whey for another use, transfer the cheese to a medium bowl, and season with salt, if desired. If using for desserts, you'll want to add little or no salt. Mold the cheese or put it in a container and cover. The cheese will keep, refrigerated, for 4 to 5 days.

WHAT TO DO WITH WHEY

Don't dump it down the drain! It provides nourishment for indoor and outdoor plants, and has many culinary uses besides. It can be used to cook porridges or grains for salads, or to serve as a broth for soup or beans. You can also add it to smoothies or simply drink it over ice.

Marinated Fresh Cheese

Here's another easy dish that illustrates how tasty foods from a D.I.Y. kitchen can be. A few fresh herbs, finely chopped shallots, and some great olive oil can transform your homemade fresh cheese into an impressive appetizer. You could do the exact same thing with store-bought cheese and it would taste good; but with your own cheese, it's great. Just serve it in a small bowl with a spoon, accompanied by fresh bread, olives, and pickles; and it will disappear fast. You can also use the marinated cheese in pasta or on pizza.

TIME REQUIRED: *5 minutes active (excluding cheese preparation)*
YIELD: *½ pound; 4 to 6 servings as an appetizer*

½ pound Fresh Whole-Milk Soft Cheese (page 106)

¼ cup extra-virgin olive oil

2 teaspoons chopped fresh parsley

2 teaspoons chopped fresh mint

2 teaspoons finely chopped shallot

1 teaspoon snipped fresh chives

½ teaspoon chopped fresh thyme

Pinch of red pepper flakes

Salt

Freshly ground black pepper

Put the cheese in a small bowl and add the oil, parsley, mint, shallot, chives, thyme, and red pepper flakes. Season with salt and pepper. Stir with a fork to crumble the cheese and distribute all the flavors. Serve immediately or cover and refrigerate for 1 or 2 days.

Savory Spinach-Cheese Pie with Olive Oil Crust

A luxurious filling of spinach and sweet, milky Fresh Whole-Milk Soft Cheese encased in a crisp-tender olive oil crust makes for a special dish that will work as a light supper, a side dish, or a picnic item. For those who are intimidated by pastry crust or pie dough, this dough is easy to mix and roll out, bakes up beautifully, and won't give you any trouble at all. You can substitute chard or kale for the spinach if you like.

TIME REQUIRED: *about 45 minutes active; 1 hour passive (excluding cheese preparation)*
YIELD: *4 servings as a meal; 6 as a side dish*

OLIVE OIL CRUST

2 cups unbleached all-purpose flour

1 teaspoon kosher salt

⅓ cup extra-virgin olive oil, plus more for brushing

FILLING

¼ cup extra-virgin olive oil

1 medium yellow onion, diced

2 garlic cloves, finely chopped

3 bunches spinach (about 1 pound), washed

Salt

¼ cup chopped fresh dill

½ pound Fresh Whole-Milk Soft Cheese (page 106)

Freshly ground black pepper

Preheat the oven to 400 degrees F.

To make the crust: In a medium bowl, mix together the flour and salt. Pour in the ⅓ cup olive oil and mix with a wooden spoon until the flour is moistened. Add ⅔ cup warm water and continue to stir. With your hands, knead the dough in the bowl for a few minutes until it comes together. The dough will be soft and elastic, but not sticky. Divide it into two equal portions, one slightly larger than the other, and set both aside while you prepare the filling.

To make the filling: In a large, heavy skillet or wok over medium heat, warm the olive oil. Add the onion and cook, stirring until soft and fragrant, about 10 minutes. Add the garlic and cook for 1 to 2 minutes, until fragrant. Add the spinach and a few pinches of salt and stir until it is wilted and cooked down (you may need to add the greens gradually and let them cook down before adding more). Add the dill, stir, and continue to cook for 1 to 2 minutes, until fragrant. Transfer the spinach mixture to a colander set in the sink and drain for a few minutes, pushing down on it with the back of a wooden spoon to release excess moisture. Transfer the spinach mixture to a cutting board and chop coarsely. Transfer it to a bowl, add the cheese, and mix together until well blended, seasoning with salt and pepper.

Select a 2-quart, 2-inch-deep baking dish of any shape. On a lightly floured surface, roll out one portion of dough in the shape of the baking dish, but slightly larger. Lay it carefully in the dish, stretching and shaping it with your hands if needed, so it comes up and over the sides of the dish. Transfer the spinach-ricotta mixture to the dish, distributing it evenly over the dough. Roll out the other piece of dough in the size and shape of the dish and place it carefully over the filling so it meets the edge of the dish, stretching and shaping if needed, and trimming if it's too large. Pinch the edges to the edge of the dish to seal. Puncture the top of the crust with the tines of a fork in several places.

Transfer the pie to the oven and bake until it is brown and crisp all over, 50 minutes to 1 hour. Brush the top of the pie with oil about 15 minutes before the end of the cooking time. Cut and serve immediately or at room temperature. Cover any leftovers and refrigerate for up to 4 days, reheating in a low (250-degree-F) oven until hot.

Fresh Cheese Crêpes

The batter for these easy crêpes is enriched with the sweet, buttery homemade Fresh Whole-Milk Soft Cheese. They're great for desserts and savory preparations. For dessert, fill them with Plum-Verbena Jam (page 50), fresh fruit, Mascarpone Cheese (page 124), or caramelized apples, or simply drizzle with honey or maple syrup and Crème Fraîche (page 116). For filling savory crêpes, try cured or smoked meats and fish or roasted or grilled seasonal vegetables. If making a savory crêpe, skip the sugar. You'll need waxed paper or oiled parchment to separate the finished crêpes as you cook them.

TIME REQUIRED: *about 30 minutes active; 20 minutes passive (excluding cheese and butter preparation)*
YIELD: *8 or 9 crêpes*

1 cup whole milk

⅔ cup unbleached all-purpose flour

½ cup Fresh Whole-Milk Soft Cheese (page 106)

3 large eggs

3 tablespoons Cultured Butter (page 121) or store-bought butter, melted, plus more for cooking

1 tablespoon sugar (omit for savory crêpes)

½ teaspoon vanilla extract

Pinch of salt

Put all of the ingredients in a blender and blend until well combined, about 2 minutes. Set aside for 20 minutes to allow the flour to absorb the liquid thoroughly.

Heat a crêpe pan or an 8-inch nonstick pan with low, sloped sides over medium-high heat. Add about ½ teaspoon butter. When the butter melts, use a spatula to distribute it evenly. Pour ⅓ cup batter into the pan and swirl quickly with a few flicks of the wrist before the batter fully sets, so that the batter covers the bottom of the pan entirely. Return to the heat and cook until the edges become brown and lacy, about 2 minutes. Flip, using a small spatula and your fingers, very carefully to avoid tearing, and cook until set on the second side, 15 to 20 seconds more. Stack the crêpes between sheets of waxed paper while you finish cooking the remainder of the batter. Fill as desired and serve immediately. You can reheat them in a 250-degree-F oven wrapped in foil. Or wrap them well and store for 3 days in the refrigerator or up to 2 months in the freezer.

Fresh Pasta with Asparagus, Homemade Cheese, and Lemon

This is such a wonderful way to enjoy spring asparagus and homemade cheese! The flavors and textures combine so well, you won't believe how simple it is to make. This recipe is one that represents the principles of the D.I.Y. kitchen perfectly. Store-bought pasta and store-bought ricotta would make a fine dish, but not transformative, as this is.

TIME REQUIRED: *15 minutes active*
(excluding butter, cheese, and pasta preparation)
YIELD: *4 to 5 servings*

1 bunch (about ¾ pound) fresh, in-season medium asparagus

2 tablespoons Cultured Butter (page 121) or store-bought butter, softened

½ pound Fresh Whole-Milk Soft Cheese (page 106), drained to a moist, slightly crumbly texture

3 tablespoons chopped mixed fresh herbs (parsley, mint, chervil, savory, marjoram—anything you like)

1 lemon for zesting

1 pound Fresh Pasta (page 164) or store-bought whole-wheat fettuccini

Salt

Freshly ground black pepper

Grasp one end of each asparagus spear in each hand and bend until it snaps at its natural breaking point. Discard (or compost) the lower fibrous ends. Cut the remaining parts of the spears into bite-sized pieces. In a vegetable steamer, steam the asparagus until tender but still vibrant green, 2 to 3 minutes. Submerge it in ice water to stop the cooking, drain, and pat dry. Set aside.

Meanwhile, bring a large pot of salted water to a boil, put the softened butter in a bowl large enough to hold all the ingredients, and have the cheese, chopped herbs, and lemon ready, as this dish comes together quickly.

Add the fresh pasta to the boiling water and cook until it is tender but still chewy, 2 to 3 minutes (if using store-bought pasta, follow package instructions). Drain immediately, do not rinse, and add the pasta to the bowl with the butter. Toss to coat the pasta, and then add the cooked asparagus, cheese, and herbs to the hot pasta. Toss and season with salt and pepper. Transfer the pasta to plates. Using a Microplane, or the small holes of a cheese grater, grate lemon zest over each serving and top with a few grindings of fresh pepper. Serve immediately.

CRÈME FRAÎCHE

Crème fraîche is a wonderfully easy dairy product to make yourself. It's perfect for beginners because success is virtually guaranteed. Making your own will save you a lot of money because store-bought crème fraîche is fantastically expensive. The basic technique is simple. Just warm up a little cream, culture it, and let it sit out at room temperature until thick. Crème fraîche is one of the more versatile items in the dairy world. Spoon a little over a creamy pureed vegetable soup like Artichoke Soup (page 119), drizzle it over Sourdough Buckwheat Pancakes with Caramelized Apples (page 157), use it to top a fresh fruit cobbler, or simply dip fresh strawberries into it. Crème fraîche's other nifty trick is that it can be cooked without curdling. I like to use yogurt as the culturing agent because I generally have it around, but you could also use sour cream or buttermilk. Ultra-pasteurized cream doesn't culture properly because in pursuit of increased shelf life, it is superheated, which kills all desirable microorganisms.

TIME REQUIRED: *10 minutes active; 12 to 24 hours passive*
YIELD: *as desired*

Fresh heavy cream (not ultra-pasteurized)

1 tablespoon yogurt, buttermilk, or sour cream per cup of cream

Pour the cream into a saucepan and turn the heat to low. Heat until slightly warmer than lukewarm (95 to 100 degrees F). Stir in the culturing agent and pour the mixture into a glass jar, such as a 1-quart mason jar. Fasten the lid and shake to blend. Leave it out in a warm area of your kitchen, such as near a pilot light or on top of the stove, for 12 to 24 hours. Check every 4 hours after the initial 8 hours to see if it has thickened. Remember that it will become even thicker after refrigeration. Taste it. It should taste tangy but not sour and it should smell clean, not funky. Once it is about the thickness of pancake batter, refrigerate it and use within 5 to 7 days.

DAIRY DISCOVERY

Yogurt can be the mother culture for all the cultured dairy products in this book. If you use yogurt to make your Crème Fraîche, you can use that Crème Fraîche to create two other dairy products in this book. Whip it to make Cultured Butter (page 121), or drain it to make a tangy-style Mascarpone Cheese (page 124).

Artichoke Soup with Crème Fraîche

Once the artichokes are prepped, this creamy soup is easy and quick to make. A dollop of crème fraîche and a sprinkling of dill nicely balance the soup's richness. You can use yogurt if you don't have crème fraîche. I choose small (not baby) or medium artichokes for this. They're easier to prepare before they've had a chance to develop much of a choke or pokey thorns. Use a serrated knife to cut the tops off the artichokes. It's much safer than a chef's knife because it won't become dull and slip.

TIME REQUIRED: *about 1 hour active; 30 minutes passive (excluding crème fraîche preparation)*
YIELD: *4 servings*

1 lemon

2½ pounds artichokes (about 6 medium)

1 quart vegetable or chicken broth, or whey from drained cheese (see page 106)

1 tablespoon olive oil

1 large leek, sliced and rinsed well

2 celery ribs, diced

4 to 5 garlic cloves, finely chopped

2 tablespoons unbleached all-purpose flour

Salt

Freshly ground black pepper

Crème Fraîche (page 116) for garnish

Chopped fresh chive or chive flowers for garnish

Ready a large bowl of water and squeeze half of the lemon into it. Keep the other lemon half handy. Using a serrated knife, cut off the top 1 inch of the artichokes (work on one artichoke at a time, rubbing the cut edges with lemon as you go to prevent browning). Cut off the bottom ½ inch of the stems. Starting at the bottom of each choke, peel back each leaf and snap it off wherever it gives. Continue working your way up to the top of each artichoke, until the remaining leaves are pale green and yellow, with no dark green tips. Using a paring knife, whittle away the dark green parts of the stem, working your way up and trimming the dark green bottom of each artichoke, continuing to rub with lemon as

continued...

you work. Cut each artichoke into quarters and scrape out the furry chokes with a stainless-steel spoon. Slice each quarter into $^1/_4$-inch-thick slices and drop them into the lemon water.

In a medium saucepan over medium heat, warm the broth to a simmer.

In a large soup pot over medium heat, warm the oil. Add the leek, celery, and garlic and cook gently until soft and fragrant, about 10 minutes. Don't let the vegetables brown. Add the flour and stir for 2 minutes, without letting it brown. Slowly whisk in the warm broth and bring to a simmer. Drain the artichokes well and add them to the pot along with a little salt and pepper. Return to a simmer, lower the heat, and cover partially. Let the soup cook until the artichokes are tender, about 30 minutes.

Let the soup cool slightly and then transfer it to a blender or food processor to puree. Process in batches to avoid splattering. Return the pureed soup to the pot, warm it up, and taste for salt and pepper. Serve in warmed bowls garnished with crème fraîche and chopped chive or chive flowers. The soup can be made 2 to 3 days ahead and stored, covered, in the refrigerator.

✓TIP: *You can use this exact method and similar proportions to make any kind of pureed vegetable soup. Simply substitute the artichokes with potatoes, asparagus, sweet potatoes, broccoli, carrots, turnips, or cauliflower. You may need to adjust the amount of liquid slightly and change up the herbs and garnishes to your taste.*

Cultured Butter

Homemade cultured butter is a revelation. If you've ever had butter in France that knocked your socks off, it was probably cultured. Culturing (simply a slight souring) gives the butter a rich, cheesy-in-a-good-way taste that is tangy and complex with layers of flavor. And it's so easy to make. Culturing butter uses the same technique as crème fraîche, and then you simply chill and whip your crème fraîche. For very little effort, you'll be rewarded with a superior product, for much less money than you'd spend at a specialty store. It's also great fun to make flavored butters out of your own cultured butter. Add flaky sea salt and enjoy with bread and radishes; or add chopped anchovies and garlic to flavor grilled fish, roasted vegetables, or beans. Stirring in dried lavender makes a wonderful butter for biscuits and muffins. While the butter is still soft, simply work the flavorings in to your taste. Making small batches of butter is best because homemade butter doesn't keep as long as store-bought, though it does freeze well. This recipe can be scaled up, but a larger batch will take longer to whip.

TIME REQUIRED: *20 to 25 minutes active (excluding crème fraîche preparation)*
YIELD: *about 4 ounces*

3 cups chilled Crème Fraîche (page 116)

Salt and flavorings (optional; see headnote)

Pour the crème fraîche into a medium bowl and, using a handheld mixer on medium-low speed, begin whipping the crème fraîche as if you were making whipped cream. Stop every now and then to scrape down the sides of the bowl with a spatula. As the crème fraîche thickens, increase the speed to medium-high. When it's just past the stage of a stiff whipped cream, the crème fraîche will become yellow and separate into clumps. At this point, decrease the speed to medium-low or you run the risk of spraying buttermilk all over. After this point, the butter will quickly solidify and separate fully from the buttermilk. The whole process takes 8 to 10 minutes. When the butter seems to have given off all the buttermilk it is going to, pour off the buttermilk and save it. (It's truly delicious,

continued...

and it's also great to use for biscuits or Aunt Mil's Jam-Filled Sugar Cookies on page 53.) Push the butter against the sides of the bowl with a flexible spatula to squeeze out as much of the buttermilk as possible.

Pour clean, cool water into the bowl and work it around and into the butter with a spatula. Pour off the water. Wash the butter two or three times until the water runs clear. This step is a must, as unwashed butter will spoil quickly.

Transfer the washed butter to a sheet of parchment and work it for a minute or so with the spatula to press out any additional water. Pat dry and then use the spatula to work in any salt and flavorings. Transfer to a clean dish, cover, and refrigerate for up to 5 days. You must keep your homemade butter refrigerated or frozen, as it is more perishable than store-bought.

MASCARPONE CHEESE

Mascarpone is a sweet, luscious dairy product that I fondly think of as a cross between whipped cream and butter. It's the traditional creamy ingredient in tiramisu. You can create easy desserts with nothing but mascarpone and seasonal fresh fruit. One of my favorite combinations is mascarpone and dates drizzled with honey. You can blend mascarpone with maple syrup and cinnamon and serve over Pain Perdu (see facing page) for breakfast or dessert. It's simple to make using one of two methods: Follow the recipe below using cream of tartar, or simply drain your own Crème Fraîche for a tangier version. Truthfully, I like the sweeter version a little better, but I love the idea of repurposing crème fraîche. You need about two days advance planning for the draining and setting-up process.

TIME REQUIRED: *15 minutes active; 32 to 36 hours passive*
YIELD: *about 2½ cups or about 1¼ pounds*

3 cups heavy cream (not ultra-pasteurized; see Crème Fraîche head note, page 116)

1 cup half-and-half

¼ teaspoon cream of tartar

Pour the heavy cream and half-and-half into the top half of a double boiler. Over medium-low heat, slowly warm the mixture to 185 degrees F, stirring occasionally. When the mixture comes to temperature, sprinkle the cream of tartar over the surface and stir it in. The mixture should thicken immediately, but it won't form large, visible curds. Maintain the temperature for 5 minutes, without stirring or allowing it to boil. Let cool slightly, transfer the mixture to a nonreactive glass or ceramic bowl, and cover. Refrigerate for 8 to 12 hours, or overnight.

Line a strainer with a coffee filter or clean towel and place it over a bowl. Transfer the mascarpone to the strainer; it should be rather thick, but pourable. Cover the bowl and set in the refrigerator to drain for 24 hours. The mascarpone is now ready to use and should be enjoyed within 5 to 7 days. Transfer it to a container, cover, and refrigerate.

Pain Perdu with Maple-Cinnamon Mascarpone

French pain perdu *is translated literally to "lost bread," which is so much more romantic than American "French toast." Such a sexy term befits this extremely decadent way to use leftover bread. Serving it with homemade Mascarpone Cheese decked out with maple syrup and cinnamon elevates it to the category of special treat. Add a little fresh fruit if you like. It's great for breakfast (especially if you plan on going back to bed!) and dessert, too.*

TIME REQUIRED: *30 minutes active; 1 hour passive (excluding bread, butter, and mascarpone preparation)*
YIELD: *2 breakfast servings; 4 dessert servings*

½ cup whole milk

¼ cup heavy cream

¼ cup sugar

1 large egg, beaten

½ teaspoon vanilla extract

4 thick slices day-old Half-Wheat Sourdough Bread (page 145) or Sourdough Cornmeal–Pumpkin Seed Bread (page 156) or purchased bread

2 tablespoons Cultured Butter (page 121) or store-bought butter

½ cup Mascarpone Cheese (facing page)

2 teaspoons maple syrup

½ teaspoon ground cinnamon

Fresh fruit (optional)

In a shallow casserole, whisk together the milk, cream, sugar, egg, and vanilla until the sugar is dissolved. Add the bread, arranging it in a single layer. Let the bread sit, turning occasionally, until it absorbs as much of the custard as it will hold, about 1 hour.

In a large, cast-iron skillet over medium heat, melt the butter. When the pan is hot and sizzling, but not smoking, add the custard-soaked bread slices. Cook on each side until dark brown on the outside and custardy but set on the inside, about 5 minutes per side. Remove from the pan and blot on paper towels.

Whisk together the mascarpone, maple syrup, and cinnamon and serve on top of the warm pain perdu, with fresh fruit, if desired.

CHAPTER FOUR

BREADS, CEREALS, AND GRAINS

SOCIETIES FROM PRIMITIVE TIMES onward have turned whole grains into flours and fermented them to make bread, before bread machines and stand-up mixers were even invented. Whole grains cooked into nourishing porridges have been staples in diets worldwide. Grocery store breads and crackers and most breakfast cereals are heavily processed, over-packaged, and filled with chemicals and additives. Our food system has taken simple foods and made them complicated, less tasty, and certainly less healthful than they once were. If our ancestors could bake breads, tortillas, and other flatbreads, we certainly can in our well-equipped modern kitchens.

You don't really need a lot of the specialized equipment sold in kitchen stores. In this chapter, you'll learn how to start a sourdough sponge from scratch, maintain it, and use it for a variety of breads, pancakes, and pizza. Create a customized granola that you'll look forward to eating for breakfast every day. Enhance your meals with freshly made tortillas. Make better crackers than you could ever buy—for pennies.

Easy recipes for using your tortillas in enchiladas, quesadillas, and chilaquiles; sandwich ideas for your home-baked bread; seasonal pizza toppings; and hot cereals with alternative whole grains round out the chapter.

CORN TORTILLAS

The traditional from-scratch way to make tortillas is to buy field corn, soak it in slaked lime, wash it thoroughly, and then grind it by hand into fresh masa. In an effort to make this recipe accessible to everyone, I've called for masa harina. It will yield tortillas that are vastly superior to grocery store tortillas for relatively little work. Masa harina is a flour made from dried masa. You can sometimes buy fresh masa made the traditional way from Latin American grocery stores. If you find fresh masa, make sure you get it plain, not preparada, which is for tamales. Also, check if it was made from masa harina. If it was, don't bother. You may as well make your own. The Maseca brand is widely available and produces consistently good tortillas. I wish I could find a good organic or local brand of masa harina. I've tried a few other types and keep coming back to Maseca for its dependability.

You will need a tortilla press and a heavy cast-iron skillet or comal. The metal tortilla presses are lightweight and affordable. Look in a Latin American grocery store or on page 227 for sources. Be sure to read the Tips for Tortilla Success (page 131) before starting.

TIME REQUIRED: *about 45 minutes active*
YIELD: *twelve 6-inch tortillas*

1½ cups masa harina	¼ teaspoon kosher salt

In a medium bowl, mix together the masa harina and salt. Add 1 cup of warm water and begin mixing with your hands. The dough should be moist and smooth, like Play-Doh. It should stick together easily when pressed but not be too wet. Add more water as needed, 1 tablespoon at a time.

Form the dough into 12 equal balls, about 1 ounce each. Lay them on a plate and cover them with a damp towel.

Get your tortilla press ready. Heat a cast-iron skillet or comal over medium-high heat. Pick up one of the masa balls and press it between your palms to flatten it slightly. Place it in the tortilla press between the plastic. Press the tortilla

continued...

firmly, but not as far as the press will go. You will need to experiment with the proper thickness. Overly thick tortillas are harder to work with and can overpower a dish. Overly thin tortillas are difficult to peel off the plastic. The tortilla should be about 6 inches in diameter.

Gently peel the tortilla off the plastic and lay it carefully in the hot pan with a sweeping motion of the hand. Cook it for 45 seconds to 1 minute, and then flip it over with a spatula. It should have small brown spots and look dry, but not cracked. Cook the second side for 30 to 45 seconds. Flip again and lightly tap the surface of the tortilla all over 4 or 5 times with your fingertips. This creates tiny pockets that make for lighter, more delicious tortillas. Cook for 15 seconds more. Turn again and tap the other side, cooking for another 15 seconds. The tortilla should smell like toasty corn and have a dull surface. Nestle each tortilla in a clean towel-lined basket to keep warm. You should be able to get a rhythm going in which you are forming one tortilla while cooking another. You may need to adjust the heat under the skillet, now and then, while you work. Use the tortillas immediately or let them cool, wrap well, and refrigerate for up to 1 week, or freeze for 2 months.

TIPS FOR TORTILLA SUCCESS

I use the method I learned from the Oaxacan women I worked with at the Jimtown Store in Healdsburg, California. They knew tricks that you won't find on a bag of masa harina.

Please note that when adding water, the amount will vary with the weather conditions. I usually find that the package instructions don't call for enough water. I end up using more or less equal parts water and masa harina.

Place a small bowl of water nearby to dip your hands in as you form the tortillas. It helps keep the masa from sticking and is a good way to work more water into the dough if it is too dry.

Don't use plastic wrap to line your tortilla press, it's too thin and difficult to work with. Use a produce bag or resealable bag, cut into one large sheet. It can be wiped off and reused until it tears.

Pinto Bean and Sweet Potato Enchiladas with All-Purpose Red Chili Sauce

This is a good use for your homemade Corn Tortillas and All-Purpose Red Chili Sauce. This dish can easily be made vegan if you omit the cheese garnish. You can also vary the vegetables however you like, using whatever's in season. Corn, summer or winter squash, and greens with cheese or potatoes are all good candidates. Of course, you can always go traditional with shredded chicken or leftover Texas-Style Barbecued Brisket (page 39).

TIME REQUIRED: *30 minutes active; 40 minutes passive (excluding sauce, tortillas, cheese, and bean preparation)*

YIELD: *4 to 6 servings*

1 pound deep-orange sweet potatoes (such as Garnet), peeled and cut into ½-inch pieces

2 tablespoons olive oil

½ teaspoon salt

¼ teaspoon whole cumin seeds

1 recipe All-Purpose Red Chili Sauce (page 70)

2 teaspoons vegetable oil

12 Corn Tortillas (page 128)

About 1 cup cooked pinto beans, drained (see bean cooking tips on page 87)

Fresh Whole-Milk Soft Cheese (page 106) or store-bought feta or queso fresco for garnish (optional)

Fresh cilantro leaves for garnish

Preheat the oven to 400 degrees F.

In a small bowl, toss the sweet potatoes with the olive oil, salt, and cumin. Lay them out in a single layer on a baking sheet and roast until browned and soft, 20 to 25 minutes. Remove from the oven and set aside. Leave the oven on.

Ladle $^2/_3$ cup of the chili sauce into the bottom of a casserole dish large enough to accommodate 12 enchiladas (a 9-by-13-inch dish works well).

In a small, heavy skillet over medium-low heat, warm about $^1/_2$ teaspoon of the vegetable oil. Add the tortillas one at a time, turning once to warm and soften them so they are pliable enough to roll, adding more oil as needed. If you are using freshly made, still-warm tortillas, you can skip this step.

Fill each tortilla with 1 heaping tablespoon of beans and 1 heaping tablespoon of sweet potato cubes. Roll and transfer it to the casserole dish, arranging each enchilada, seam-side down, on top of the sauce in a single layer. Pour the remaining sauce over the enchiladas, covering them completely and distributing it evenly. You may have leftover sweet potatoes. Sprinkle them over the top of the enchiladas or reserve them for use in one of the grain salads in the Great Salad Toss-Up Guide (page 92). Cover the casserole with aluminum foil and bake until warmed through, 10 to 15 minutes.

Garnish each serving with fresh cheese (if using) and cilantro leaves.

Chilaquiles

Every culture has devised ways to use leftover staple grain products, as in the Pain Perdu with Maple-Cinnamon Mascarpone (page 125). In Italy, there are innumerable bread salads and soups; in Asia, it's fried rice; in Mexico, it's chilaquiles, usually served for breakfast. If you should find yourself in the enviable position of having leftover Corn Tortillas, there is no better use for them than this. This recipe provides basic quantities and technique, but it is within the spirit of the dish to vary it by using up little bits of odds and ends you have in your refrigerator, like cooked beans, leftover Mustard and Bourbon–Glazed Pork Roast (page 36), or Texas-Style Barbecued Brisket (page 39). You can also drizzle a little Crème Fraîche (page 116) on the Chilaquiles as a garnish. Of course, you can also make this with store-bought tortillas, but the quantities are slightly different, as commercial tortillas are generally larger. These are lovely with Hibiscus Tea (page 225) or Horchata (page 222).

TIME REQUIRED: *10 minutes active
(excluding tortillas, salsa, and cheese preparation)*
YIELD: *4 to 6 servings*

8 large eggs

Salt

Freshly ground black pepper

12 Corn Tortillas (page 128), or 8 store-bought corn tortillas

⅓ cup vegetable oil, plus 1 teaspoon

½ red onion, thinly sliced

2 cups Simple Tomato Salsa (page 72) or Avocado-Tomatillo Salsa (page 71)

2 to 3 ounces Fresh Whole-Milk Soft Cheese (page 106) or store-bought feta or queso fresco for garnish

Fresh cilantro sprigs for garnish

In a large bowl, beat the eggs until smooth and add about $\frac{1}{2}$ teaspoon salt and $\frac{1}{4}$ teaspoon pepper.

Stack the tortillas three or four high, and cut them into six to eight wedges.

In a large cast-iron skillet over medium heat, warm the $\frac{1}{3}$ cup of the oil. Add the onion, and cook, stirring, until it begins to soften and brown, 5 to 8 minutes. Increase the heat to medium-high and add the tortilla wedges. Cook, stirring occasionally, until they are browned and crispy. Pour in the salsa. Be careful—it splatters. Stir to blend with the chips. Move the tortillas and salsa to one side of the pan, add the remaining teaspoon of oil to the empty side of the pan, and pour in the eggs. Scramble the eggs for a few minutes, until nearly cooked. Stir the eggs into the tortillas. Turn off the heat, season with salt and pepper, and serve immediately, garnished with fresh cheese and cilantro.

FLOUR TORTILLAS

I love flour tortillas. I grew up eating them as an after-school snack with grated orange cheese or margarine and cinnamon-sugar. Those memories are hard to shake. Just the same, I pretty much gave up on eating flour tortillas after reading the labels on the ones sold in grocery stores. For some reason, I thought they were difficult to make. Not true! These work beautifully and cook up delightfully with a tender flakiness. I like to add a little wheat flour for structure and nutrition. You'll barely be able to resist tearing through them right out of the skillet. Resist you must, though, because they make wonderful Zucchini and Mushroom Quesadillas (page 139). You'll want leftovers, too, for reheating and eating with a little Cultured Butter and a sprinkling of cinnamon-sugar. The dough is easy to work with so there is no need to use a tortilla press.

TIME REQUIRED: *45 minutes active; 30 minutes passive (excluding butter preparation)*
YIELD: *twelve 8-inch tortillas*

2½ cups unbleached all-purpose flour

½ cup whole-wheat flour

1½ teaspoons kosher salt

1 teaspoon baking powder

2 tablespoons vegetable oil

2 tablespoons Cultured Butter (page 121) or store-bought butter, softened

In a large bowl, mix together the all-purpose flour, wheat flour, salt, and baking powder. Add the oil and butter and mix with your hands, rubbing the fat into the flour with your fingertips. Pour in 1¼ cups warm water a little at a time and knead for 2 or 3 minutes in the bowl. The dough should be soft and pliable but not sticky. Let the dough rest for 15 or 20 minutes under a damp towel.

Form the dough into 12 equal balls, about 2 ounces each. Let rest for about 10 minutes (longer is okay if covered with a damp towel).

Heat a dry cast-iron skillet over medium-high heat.

On a lightly floured board or counter, flatten one dough ball slightly with your palm and, using a rolling pin, roll it out into a thin circle 8 inches in diameter. When the skillet is hot, but not smoking, gently peel the tortilla off the counter and carefully place it in the pan. Cook for 1 minute, and then flip it over with a spatula. It should have small brown spots. Cook for 1 minute on the other side. Nestle the cooked tortillas in a clean towel as you finish cooking the rest. Once you get a rhythm going, you should be able to roll out one while cooking another. The dough is easy to work with and shouldn't give you trouble. You may need to adjust the heat under the pan if you notice the tortillas cooking either too quickly or too slowly. Use the tortillas immediately or let them cool, wrap well, and refrigerate for up to 1 week or freeze for 2 months.

Zucchini and Mushroom Quesadillas

Ordinary vegetables become extraordinary when tucked into homemade flour tortillas. Vary these to your liking or according to the season. You can make them with beans, chicken, winter squash, or any other number of seasonal vegetables. Use store-bought cheese if you're not feeling ambitious enough to make your own, but if you at least make the Simple Tomato Salsa or the Avocado-Tomatillo Salsa and the Flour Tortillas, you're in for a real treat.

TIME REQUIRED: *about 45 minutes active*
(excluding salsa, cheese, and tortilla preparation)
YIELD: *4 servings*

3½ to 4 tablespoons vegetable oil

½ yellow or white onion, sliced

About ¾ pound mushrooms of your choice, sliced

2 medium zucchini, cut in half lengthwise and sliced

2 garlic cloves, finely chopped

1½ teaspoons dried Mexican oregano, crumbled

Salt

Freshly ground black pepper

8 Flour Tortillas (page 136) or store-bought tortillas

About 1¼ cups Fresh Whole-Milk Soft Cheese (page 106) or store-bought grating cheese or queso fresco

About 1½ cups Simple Tomato Salsa (page 72) or Avocado-Tomatillo Salsa (page 71), plus more for serving

Fresh cilantro leaves for garnish

continued...

In a medium, heavy skillet over medium heat, warm 2 tablespoons of the oil. Add the onion and cook until wilted and fragrant, about 8 minutes. Add the mushrooms, zucchini, garlic, oregano, a pinch or two of salt, and a couple of grindings of pepper. Cook, stirring, until the mushrooms are brown and soft, about 10 minutes. Taste and correct the seasoning for salt. The vegetables can be prepared from several hours to 2 days ahead and refrigerated.

Lay the tortillas out on a flat surface and distribute the filling among them, arranging it on one side of each tortilla so they can easily be folded over. Sprinkle the cheese on top of the vegetables, distributing it evenly among the tortillas. Spoon the salsa on top of the filling and cheese, distributing it evenly.

Heat a heavy, well-seasoned, cast-iron skillet over medium heat and add just a whisper of oil—about 1 teaspoon. Fold the quesadillas over and cook them, two at a time, until brown and slightly crisp, and the filling is warmed through, about 3 minutes per side. Keep the cooked quesadillas warm in a low (250-degree-F) oven while you finish cooking the remaining ones, adding more oil as needed. Serve immediately with more salsa on the side and a garnish of cilantro.

SOURDOUGH STARTER

This is a method anyone can use anywhere to make his or her own sourdough starter from scratch. It's true that sourdough bread from California will taste different from sourdough bread in North Carolina, because different areas have different types of wild yeasts and organisms, but every part of the world has them.

TIME REQUIRED: *10 minutes per day over about 1 week*

Start with equal parts flour and water. I like to start with 4 ounces whole-wheat flour and 4 ounces warm water. After your starter gets going, you can use half unbleached white bread flour and half whole-wheat, all-white, or other types of flours. Starting with whole wheat is good because it ferments more efficiently than white flour.

In a medium glass bowl (which I prefer) or hard, food-grade plastic container, stir together the flour and water and cover with a tea towel, fastened with a rubber band to keep out fruit flies. Leave it out at room temperature. The starter needs to breathe, so don't cover it with a tight lid unless you are keeping it dormant in the refrigerator.

After 24 hours, check it for bubbles and a fermented aroma. It will probably take 2 to 3 days to begin to ferment.

Each day, discard half the starter (and compost it) and stir in 4 ounces warm water and 4 ounces flour. It's easier to mix if you add the water first. Cover and let sit.

Leave it at room temperature and feed the starter once a day for approximately 1 week before baking with it.

Keep your starter covered in the refrigerator between baking sessions. See page 151 for instructions on feeding in preparation for a bake.

HOW TO TELL IF YOUR STARTER
IS READY TO BAKE WITH

It should be bubbly and have a good beery, floury aroma. If nothing happens after a week, you may need to help it along. Many people use raisins (unsulfured) because of the active wild yeasts on their surfaces. Just throw a few raisins into your starter and discard them after the starter gets going. I have never needed to do this, though.

If the starter is bad, there will be no mistaking it. It will smell absolutely revolting. If this happens, it just means some bad bacteria got into it. Discard it and start over. This is a rare occurrence.

Once the starter is colonized by good bacteria, you won't need to worry about bad stuff taking over because the bad bacteria don't stand a chance in an active, healthy starter.

Once you have a good healthy starter, the only way to kill or harm it is to stop feeding it and leave it out.

If you need to leave town for longer than 2 or 3 weeks, feed your starter with a larger percentage of flour to water to make it very dry. It should be crumbly. Keep it refrigerated for up to 1 month, or freeze it if you must be away longer. When you return, it will take a few daily regular feedings with a higher proportion of water to bring it back up, so plan a couple of extra feedings before baking.

Try to use your starter every 2 weeks or more often. If you go longer though, don't worry. Sometimes you'll just need an extra feeding before baking. You'll get to know your starter and its particular behavior over time. I have left mine unattended with no special treatment in the refrigerator for as long as a month and a half and after a couple of extra feedings to increase its activity it was fine.

Half-Wheat Sourdough Bread

Baking bread requires a little advance thought and planning, so read the note on feeding your starter in preparation for baking before you begin this recipe.

This recipe and the Sourdough Cornmeal–Pumpkin Seed Bread (page 156) were both developed in consultation with artisan baker Eduardo Morell (see page 152). Many of Eduardo's loaves have this loaf's identical ratio of wheat to white flour, providing a nice balance of tenderness and flavor. This loaf can be baked in one of two ways: in a one-pound loaf pan or free-form in a closed ceramic bread baker, sometimes called a cloche. Instructions for both follow.

Measurements are given in weights and cups. I highly recommend buying a kitchen scale to ensure bread success.

After a few baking sessions, you will learn to adjust to your kitchen's atmosphere and your preference. Be aware that moister dough is more difficult to shape but will produce a loaf with a more desirable, open crumb. Add more flour and your dough will be easier to shape, but will yield a denser bread. Beginners can start with a slightly greater percentage of flour to water and work up to moister dough as they become more adept at shaping.

TIME REQUIRED: *about 40 minutes active; 7 hours passive (excluding starter preparation)*
YIELD: *one 1-pound loaf*

---

11 ounces (about 1⅓ cups) slightly warmer than lukewarm water (about 100 degrees F)

5 ounces (about ⅔ cup) recently fed and activated Sourdough Starter (page 141)

8 ounces (about 1¾ cups) wheat flour

7 ounces (about 1⅔ cups) unbleached bread flour

1½ teaspoons kosher salt

Vegetable oil or rice flour for pan

Pour the water into a large bowl and add the starter. Mix with your hands to dissolve the starter in the water.

Have a small bowl of plain water handy for dipping your hands into. It keeps the dough from sticking.

continued....

In another bowl, mix together the flours and salt. Add to the water-starter mixture. Mix in the flour with one hand, using a folding motion from the outside of the bowl inward, turning the bowl with your other hand as you go. Scrape down the sides with a flexible bowl scraper, wetting both it and your hands as needed. This will take 3 to 5 minutes. Cover with a towel and let the dough sit in the bowl for 5 minutes.

Using the same outward to inward motion with your hands, knead the dough in the bowl for an additional 5 minutes, dipping your hands in water as necessary. Cover the dough and let sit for 5 minutes.

Repeat, kneading for 5 minutes.

You may use a mixer, but go slowly as it is easy to overwork the dough. Eduardo describes it like overworking a muscle. Too much or too vigorous mixing can break the gluten strands and prevent the bread from rising properly.

Cover the bowl with a towel and let it sit in a warm place for 3 hours. This is called the bulk rise. About halfway through the bulk rise, do a quick fold, using the outside to inside movement (about four turns). If it's a cold day, turn your oven on for a minute and then turn it off and put the dough inside to finish the bulk rise.

If it's a hot day, the whole process will just go much faster and your bulk rise can take as little as $2\frac{1}{2}$ hours.

Dump the bulk dough onto a well-floured board or counter. Sprinkle a little flour on top. When you need to move the dough, use your flexible scraper to do so.

You'll want to use the least amount of flour possible when shaping because unhydrated flour in the middle of the dough can cause large holes.

Using both hands, grasp the sides of the dough and stretch and pull it gently into a slight rectangle. Grasp the short ends of the rectangle and fold each side in toward the middle. Give the dough a quarter turn, stretch it again, and fold into the middle. Using your scraper, turn the dough mass over so the folded ends are underneath. Spin the dough with one hand and tuck the dough underneath with the other, stretching the top gently into a round. Let it sit for 5 minutes.

continued . . . .

If baking in a loaf pan, brush the pan with oil. If using a ceramic bread baker, you will be making a free-form loaf. For free-form loaves, line a glass dish or bowl with a tea or thin kitchen towel and dust with rice flour. You may use regular flour, but rice flour prevents sticking much better.

To shape a loaf for the loaf pan, after the preshaped loaf has rested undisturbed for 5 minutes, turn it over and pull and stretch it gently into a rectangle. Fold each of the narrower sides in toward one another and then grasp the top with both hands and make two folds down and inward, on either side, like an envelope, forming a triangle whose tip is on the top edge of the rectangle.

Grasp this top point of the loaf and pull it toward you to form a horizontal cylinder-shaped loaf. Work your way slowly along the length of the dough, tucking and stretching gently with your hands to make a seam on the underside of the loaf. Push lightly on the loaf to smooth out any air bubbles.

Roll the loaf slightly forward so the seam is just visible on the underside of the loaf. Using the heel of your hand along the length of the seam, push the dough gently but firmly against the work surface using the weight of your hand to seal it, but not smash the loaf. With the scraper in one hand, and the dough in the other, gently lift the dough and turn it seam-side down into the prepared loaf pan. Cover with a towel and let it sit for 3 hours for its second rise. If you want to bake the next day, you can leave the loaf out for 30 minutes to 1 hour for its second rise and then transfer it to the refrigerator for 8 to 24 hours to retard the fermentation. In this case, remove it from the refrigerator 1 hour before baking.

For a free-form loaf, turn the preshaped loaf over after it has rested for 5 minutes so that the folds are now on top. Stretch the dough out a little and then tuck the dough inward toward the top into a round, much like the preshaped loaf. Turn it over and put it in the towel-lined dish to sit for 3 hours for its second rise.

Preheat the oven to 475 degrees F.

With a sharp serrated knife or razor blade dipped in vegetable oil make two or three slashes in the top of the loaf to allow it to expand evenly in the oven.

continued...

If baking in a loaf pan, you will need to introduce steam into the process in order to create a desirable crisp, brown crust. The best method is to preheat a cast-iron skillet or oven-safe saucepan in the bottom of the oven or on a rack below where you will be baking the bread. Put the bread in the oven and, working quickly, pour about 1 cup of cool tap water into the preheated skillet or saucepan and close the oven door.

If baking free-form in a closed ceramic bread baker, the bread will create its own steam and you do not need to add water. However, you must preheat the bread baker as you preheat the oven. Remove the preheated baker from the oven carefully, open the lid, and quickly transfer the bread from its flour-lined towel into the bread baker, seam-side down. Close the baker's lid and return it to the oven.

Bake for 15 minutes. If using a ceramic baker, remove the dome lid at this point. Lower the oven temperature to 425 degrees F and bake the bread until it is dark brown all over, another 20 minutes. Remove the bread from the loaf pan or bread baker, place it directly on the rack, and continue to bake until the bread feels light when lifted and sounds hollow when you knock gently on the bottom of the loaf, an additional 5 minutes. Removing the bread to the rack will give it a crisp crust all over. Remove the bread to a cooling rack and let it cool completely before cutting and serving. It will keep for 2 days stored in a paper bag at room temperature. For longer storage, slice the bread and keep it in a resealable bag in the freezer, removing the desired number of pieces, as needed.

✓TROUBLESHOOTING TIP: *If the bread comes out sour and dense, the second rising was too long. If the bread rises too quickly in the oven and explodes, the second rising was too short.*

SOURDOUGH FEEDING AND BREAD BAKING TIMELINE

Home-baked sourdough bread requires a lead time of 34 to 36 hours. Most of this is inactive time, but it does require advance planning. Decide when you want the bread to be ready and count back from there.

Let's say you want freshly baked bread for Saturday dinner. You'll need 1 hour baking and cooling time, 3 hours of second rise (or up to 24 hours), 15 minutes of shaping time, 3 hours of bulk rise, and 30 minutes of mixing and kneading (total = 7¾ hours). You also need to feed your starter at least once, preferably twice, after removing it from the refrigerator and before baking.

SAMPLE SCHEDULE

For bread on Saturday night around 7 P.M.:

Friday morning: Remove the starter from the refrigerator.

Friday, 6 P.M.: Feed the starter when you get home from your day, following instructions on page 141.

Feed again before bed (or around 11 P.M.). You can bake bread after only one feeding, but you'll have better texture and flavor if you feed it twice. For instance, you could remove the starter from the fridge on Friday evening and feed it before bed and then proceed the next morning.

Saturday, between 10 and 11 A.M.: Start mixing the dough.

Follow instructions for Half-Wheat Sourdough Bread (page 145) or Sourdough-Cornmeal Pumpkin Seed Bread (page 156).

NOTES: *A kitchen scale is invaluable for baking bread, leading to much greater precision.*

Flexible plastic bowl scraper or hand spatulas will make you feel like a pro. They help you scrape wet dough out of the bowl and maneuver it expertly once it's on the board.

EDUARDO MORELL'S BREAD–
IT'S GOT SOUL

"Artisan" is a term used by supermarkets to add gourmet cachet to loaves of mostly white bread full of additives and often additions of "gourmet" flavors like Cheddar cheese and jalapeño. Real artisan bread is made by hand using a wild sourdough starter and plenty of time to help it develop complex flavor, an open crumb, crisp crust, and chewy texture. Real artisan bread includes flour, salt, water, and sourdough starter. You can add fresh herbs, seeds, or nuts, if you like, but you don't need anything else.

Eduardo Morell runs one of the smallest commercial artisan bakeries in the San Francisco Bay Area. Working out of a wood-burning oven in the kitchen of an old army barracks at Headlands Center for the Arts near Sausalito, California, Eduardo bakes a variety of real sourdough breads under the name Morell's Bread. He makes ciabatta, multigrain, spelt, sesame, rye, and rosemary breads, along with bagels and scones—all from a sourdough starter with the highest-quality locally milled flours. This is real bread, made slowly and carefully the way it has been for centuries. It's crusty, flavorful, and full of nutrition and heart—a far cry from that puffy white loaf you'll find in the bakery aisle of your local grocery store.

With the help of his assistant, Megan Launer, Eduardo bakes about 400 loaves a week, staying up into the wee hours, and then heading into Berkeley to sell at both the Thursday and the Saturday farmers' markets. He bakes his bread himself, transports it himself, and sells it himself, qualifying as a true micro producer. I am so lucky to know him and thankful that he shared his skills with me for this book. The two sourdough breads you find in this book were baked using his methods with a starter made from scratch, all scaled down and adapted for the home cook.

The Headlands Center for the Arts is a magical place. Situated on a windswept hillside in the Golden Gate National Recreation Area, the buildings that were once army housing and a mess hall now host artists from all over the world in a variety of disciplines. The remodel of the kitchen was commissioned by designer Ann Hamilton in 1989. She created a true community-gathering place to facilitate the exchange of ideas and welcome both the artists and the public to the space. Part of her vision included a hearth, so she enlisted renowned builder Alan Scott to build the wood-burning oven that serves as the heart of the kitchen.

Everyone who walks into the kitchen at Headlands immediately feels its power. It draws you in and makes you want to stay forever. That's how it happened for Eduardo. He came in 1998 and went from intern to chef to kitchen manager to baker. Along the way, he learned traditional baking skills from a French baker who was baking there before him. He developed his own techniques over the years and now, in addition to selling his breads at the farmers' markets, he supplies the kitchen with bread for artist dinners and public programs.

Sandwich Inspiration Guide

You might never want to buy another sandwich again. By combining the two basic breads in this chapter, the condiments and spreads, homemade cheese, butter, and pickles, and, occasionally, a few store-bought ingredients, you can create sandwich combinations for every mood, including moods you never anticipated. Here are some combinations that I like. You'll come up with more on your own.

HALF-WHEAT SOURDOUGH BREAD (PAGE 145)

- Ajvar (page 74), Easy Yogurt Cheese (page 99), and Pickled Kohlrabi and Turnips with Cardamom (page 202)

- Fig-Rosemary Jam (page 55) and Mustard and Bourbon–Glazed Pork Roast (page 36)

- Grainy Prepared Mustard (page 32), Mustard and Bourbon–Glazed Pork Roast (page 36), and Garlicky Cucumber Pickle Relish (page 208)

- Texas-Style Barbecued Brisket with Spicy Barbecue Sauce (page 39)

- Roasted Peanut Butter (page 68) and Simple Wild Sauerkraut (page 186)—try it! I'm serious!

- Meyer Lemon and Parsley Aioli (page 43) and store-bought canned wild salmon

SOURDOUGH CORNMEAL– PUMPKIN SEED BREAD (PAGE 156)

- Fresh Whole-Milk Soft Cheese (page 106) and Persimmon Spice Butter (page 60)

- Fresh Whole-Milk Soft Cheese (page 106) and Bread and Butter Pickles (page 200)

- Raw Almond Butter (page 63) and Plum-Verbena Jam (page 50)

- Mustard and Bourbon–Glazed Pork Roast (page 36) and Persimmon-Spice Butter (page 60)

- BLT with Meyer Lemon and Parsley Aioli (page 43)

- Egg salad made with Meyer Lemon Aioli (page 43) and Garlicky Cucumber Pickle Relish (page 208)

- Texas-Style Barbecued Brisket (page 39) and Ajvar (page 74)

- Grilled Cheese and Wild Salvadoran Curtido (page 198)

Sourdough Cornmeal–Pumpkin Seed Bread

I love the crunch of cornmeal and the nutty flavor of pumpkin seeds combined. Both work well in this sourdough loaf. This is lovely sandwich bread and is even better toasted. Enjoy it for breakfast with homemade Cultured Butter (page 121) and local honey or Plum-Verbena Jam (page 50). The replacement of some of the wheat flour with cornmeal makes a relatively moist dough. For this reason, I recommend baking this bread in a one-pound loaf pan to contain it rather than freeform.

TIME REQUIRED: *about 40 minutes active; 7 hours passive (excluding Sourdough Starter preparation)*

YIELD: *one 1-pound loaf*

11 ounces (about 1⅓ cups) slightly warmer than lukewarm water (about 100 degrees F)

5 ounces (about ⅔ cup) recently fed and activated Sourdough Starter (page 141)

8 ounces (about 1¾ cups) unbleached bread flour

5 ounces (about ¾ cup) yellow cornmeal

2 ounces (a scant ½ cup) wheat flour

2 teaspoons kosher salt

⅓ cup (2 ounces) pumpkin seeds, lightly toasted

Follow the instructions for mixing, forming, and baking the Half-Wheat Sourdough Bread (page 145), mixing the cornmeal in with both flours and adding the pumpkin seeds when you add the dry ingredients to the water and starter.

Sourdough Buckwheat Pancakes with Caramelized Apples and Crème Fraîche

These are wonderful, special-occasion pancakes that somehow manage to taste both decadent and healthful at the same time. Serve them drizzled with maple syrup or Plum-Verbena Jam and homemade Crème Fraîche.

TIME REQUIREMENT: *45 minutes active*
(excluding crème fraîche, butter, jam, and sourdough starter preparation)
YIELD: *about 24 three-inch pancakes; 4 to 6 servings*

2 tablespoons Cultured Butter (page 121) or store-bought butter

2 tablespoons lightly packed brown sugar

½ teaspoon ground cinnamon

1 apple, chopped into ¼-inch pieces (about 1½ cups)

1⅓ cups room-temperature Sourdough Starter (page 141), fed the night before or at least 4 hours ahead (see page 151 for feeding instructions)

1¼ cups milk

2 large eggs, separated

½ teaspoon vanilla extract

1 cup unbleached all-purpose flour

⅓ cup buckwheat flour

1 tablespoon granulated sugar

Salt

Vegetable oil for the pan

Crème Fraîche (page 116) for serving

Plum-Verbena Jam (page 50) or maple syrup for serving

In a small, heavy skillet over medium heat, warm the butter, add the brown sugar and cinnamon, and stir to melt. Add the apple and cook, stirring occasionally, until soft, brown, and caramelized, about 10 minutes. Set aside to cool.

In a large bowl, whisk together the sourdough starter, milk, egg yolks, and vanilla. Add the flours, granulated sugar, a pinch of salt, and the cooled apples, leaving some aside for garnish, if desired, and mix with a wooden spoon to blend.

In a medium bowl, using a handheld electric mixer, beat the egg whites until medium-firm peaks form. Fold them gently into the batter, distributing the egg whites evenly, without overmixing.

continued...

Heat a large, well-seasoned, cast-iron skillet over medium-high heat and, using a paper towel, rub a little oil on its surface to coat it lightly. Test the heat level by drizzling a few drops of batter into the skillet. They should sizzle and begin to brown on the edges immediately. When the skillet is ready, ladle in 2 to 3 ounces of batter for each pancake. You should be able to cook three or four pancakes at a time. Cook the pancakes until bubbles form along the edges and the edges dry, about 2 minutes. Flip them over and cook the other sides until brown. Keep the finished pancakes warm in a low (250-degree-F) oven while you complete the cooking process. Serve the pancakes with crème fraîche and Plum-Verbena Jam. Garnish with the reserved caramelized apple pieces.

Sourdough Pizza Crust

Though I'm big on making do in the kitchen and avoiding single-use tools and equipment, pizza is the one food item for which I recommend investing in the proper specialized tools—in this case, both a wooden peel and a baking stone. Neither one is terribly expensive, and both are necessary to making crisp, thin-crusted pizza. It's also important to remember that making great pizza is a craft, just like making great bread. The variables in your kitchen—oven calibration, climate, moisture in the air, type of flour, water, and how you work the dough—will all contribute to the outcome. So if your pizza isn't perfect the first time out, try and try again. Your "mistakes" will still be delicious.

TIME REQUIRED: *20 to 50 minutes active (depending on toppings); 3 to 5 hours passive (excluding sourdough starter preparation)*
YIELD: *2 approximately 15-inch pizzas*

1 cup room-temperature Sourdough Starter (page 141), fed that morning or at least 4 hours ahead (see page 151 for feeding instructions)

3 cups unbleached all-purpose or bread flour

2 tablespoons olive oil

½ teaspoon kosher salt

Cornmeal for dusting

Desired toppings (see Guide to Pizzas Through the Seasons, page 163)

Mix together ¾ cup warm water and the starter and stir to dissolve the starter. Add the flour, oil, and salt, and mix with a rubber spatula. Add more water as needed until the dough is pliable. Continue to mix. Dip your hands in water and knead the dough in the bowl for 5 minutes. The dough will be quite sticky, but if you keep dipping your hands in water, it will prevent the dough from sticking to your hands. Cover the bowl, put it in a warm place, and let it rise for 3 to 5 hours.

Preheat the oven and pizza stone to 550 degrees F.

Punch down and divide the dough into two balls. Flour a work surface generously and lay the balls down, flattening them slightly with your hands. Dust the tops with more flour. Let them rest for 10 minutes. Stretch or roll each ball out to about 15 inches and place one on a cornmeal-dusted pizza peel. Stretch until the dough covers the peel. If making a pizza without sauce, brush lightly with olive oil before topping. Top as desired. To slide the pizza onto the stone in the oven, make sure it slides easily on the peel first, then hold the peel right over the stone and jerk it back sharply with a slight upward motion of your wrist. The pizza should slide onto the stone effortlessly. If it sticks, help it along with a spatula and use a little more cornmeal next time. Bake until brown and crisp, about 10 minutes. Repeat with the other pizza round, or freeze the pizza dough, well wrapped, for up to 2 weeks. Thaw thoroughly before using.

Guide to Pizzas
Through the Seasons

Once you perfect your Sourdough Pizza Crust (page 160), you'll want to make it all the time. It's economical, easy, and fun, and everyone loves it. I like to create pizzas with the seasons from what's available in my pantry and at the farmers' market. Here are some of my favorite seasonal combos:

WINTER

- Thinly sliced boiled potatoes, sautéed chard, salami or prosciutto (optional), fontina cheese

- Sliced and roasted butternut squash, sage leaves, mushrooms, fontina cheese, mozzarella or Fresh Whole-Milk Soft Cheese (page 106). Pictured on facing page

- Sausage, Simple Wild Sauerkraut (page 186), and aged cheese such as Pecorino Romano or gouda

SPRING

- Asparagus, spring onions, and fresh pecorino or Fresh Whole-Milk Soft Cheese (page 106)

- Prosciutto or thinly sliced smoked wild salmon or trout, cooked on the pizza, and then topped with Crème Fraîche (page 116) and fresh arugula lightly dressed in olive oil after it comes out of the oven

- Roasted baby artichokes, fresh herbs, and goat cheese

SUMMER

- Corn, fresh cherry tomatoes, basil, Fresh Whole-Milk Soft Cheese (page 106) or mozzarella

- Freshly made tomato sauce, basil, and mozzarella

- Arugula, cilantro or mint pesto, sautéed summer squash, and Fresh Whole-Milk Soft Cheese (page 106) or feta

FALL

- Roasted red peppers, eggplant, olives, and Fresh Whole-Milk Soft Cheese (page 106) or feta

- Tomato sauce, sausage, and thinly sliced fennel (added after cooking); with or without cheese

- Shredded Mustard and Bourbon– Glazed Pork Roast (page 36), cooked on the pizza and then topped with Garlicky Cucumber Pickle Relish (page 208) after it comes out of the oven; no cheese

FRESH PASTA

This pasta combines the healthful, nutty characteristics of whole-wheat pasta with the crowd-pleasing traits of regular egg pasta. It's light enough to pair with delicate vegetable preparations like Fresh Pasta with Asparagus, Homemade Cheese, and Lemon (page 115) or anything with fish. For the Fresh Pasta with Cabbage, Bacon, Sage, and Brown Butter (page 167), I like to substitute buckwheat flour for the wheat flour. You may want to experiment with the ratio of wheat to white flour, depending on your sauce. You can roll and cut the pasta on a stainless-steel pasta maker or you can roll and cut the noodles by hand.

TIME REQUIRED: *35 to 50 minutes active, depending on how you roll and cut it; 20 minutes passive*
YIELD: *about 1 pound; 4 to 5 servings*

1 cup unbleached all-purpose flour, plus more for dusting	2 large eggs
½ cup whole-wheat or buckwheat flour	½ teaspoon kosher salt

In a small bowl, mix together the flours, eggs, salt, and ¼ cup water with a fork until it forms a ball. If it doesn't come together easily, dip your hands in water so the dough doesn't stick and knead the dough with your hands just until mixed. Cover with plastic wrap or a towel to prevent drying and let the dough rest for 20 minutes.

IF USING A PASTA MACHINE:

Dust a clean, flat surface with flour and then separate the pasta into six equal pieces. Flatten each portion of pasta between the palms of your hands until it is about ½ inch thick and narrow enough to fit into the pasta roller. Dust each pasta piece generously with flour. With your pasta maker set at #1 thickness, start rolling the pasta disks out, progressing through #2 and #3 and ending with #4. Use the fettuccini cutter on the pasta machine to make flat noodles. Separate the noodles and lay them out on a floured surface. If they seem sticky, dust them lightly with flour and finish rolling and cutting the remaining pasta.

continued...

TO ROLL AND CUT BY HAND:

Dust a clean, flat surface with flour and then separate the pasta into six equal pieces. Flatten each portion of pasta between the palms of your hands until it is about ½ inch thick. Using plenty of flour on both sides of the pieces of pasta, and a rolling pin, roll one of the pieces of pasta out as thinly as possible into a sheet 7 to 8 inches long and 3 to 4 inches wide. Starting on the short end of the sheet, roll the pasta up jelly-roll style. With a sharp knife, cut the roll into strips ⅓ inch wide, and unfurl the resulting noodles. Lay the noodles out on a well-floured surface, not touching, and repeat the process of rolling and cutting the remaining pieces of dough.

To cook, plunge the noodles into boiling, salted water until tender but chewy, 2 to 3 minutes. Drain and use immediately.

Fresh Pasta with Cabbage, Bacon, Sage, and Brown Butter

Rich and deeply comforting, this is a dish to make on a cold winter or crisp fall evening. It's wonderful with either the wheat or buckwheat version of Fresh Pasta. I like to make it with the buckwheat noodles because it reminds me of a classic Italian dish called pizzoccheri, *which involves cabbage, potatoes, lots of cheese, even more butter, and sage. Once the pasta is made, this dish comes together very quickly.*

TIME REQUIRED: *40 minutes active (excluding pasta and butter preparation)*
YIELD: *4 servings*

6 pieces thick-cut bacon (about 6 ounces)

½ large head cabbage (about 1 pound)

1 recipe Fresh Pasta (page 164), or about 10 ounces packaged, dry pasta

½ yellow onion, thinly sliced

3 tablespoons Cultured Butter (page 121) or store-bought butter

20 whole sage leaves

Salt

Freshly ground black pepper

Parmesan cheese for garnish

Cut the bacon crosswise into ½-inch slices.

Core the cabbage, pull off the outer leaves, and slice it into ribbons ¼ to ½ inch thick.

In a medium, heavy skillet over medium-low heat, brown the bacon in its own fat until all the fat is rendered and the bacon begins to crisp, stirring occasionally, 12 to 14 minutes. With a slotted spoon, remove the bacon to a paper towel–lined plate. Pour off all but about 2 teaspoons of the fat and refrigerate it for another use (it's great for cooking beans).

Bring a large pot of salted water to a boil. Have the pasta ready.

continued...

While waiting for the pasta water to boil, turn the heat under the skillet to medium-high, add the cabbage and onion, and cook, stirring often, until the cabbage and onion wilt and begin to brown, 7 to 10 minutes. Add the bacon and toss to mix. Turn off the heat.

In a deep pan or skillet large enough to contain all the noodles, warm the butter over medium-high heat. When the foam subsides, add the sage leaves and fry, stirring occasionally, until they become fragrant and the butter browns and develops a nutty aroma, 2 to 3 minutes. Add the cabbage, bacon, and onion mixture and toss. Set aside, off the heat, while you boil the noodles.

Plunge the noodles into the boiling water until tender but chewy, 2 to 3 minutes; drain. Do not rinse. If using dried pasta, follow the package instructions.

Add the drained pasta to the pan with the cabbage mixture. Toss to coat. Taste and correct the seasoning for salt and pepper. Serve immediately on warmed plates, shaving thin shards of Parmesan cheese over each portion with a vegetable peeler.

WHOLE-WHEAT
SESAME CRACKERS

When you first start making crackers, you might notice that your crackers taste great, but there will be something different that you can't put your finger on. It's the lack of sugar. Read the labels on even some of the "healthier" brands of store-bought crackers, and you'll find that most of them contain sugar—or worse, high-fructose corn syrup. It's sad how our tastes have become accustomed to industrialized food "products." I happen to think crackers don't need sugar, and when you taste these and the Cornmeal, Parmesan, and Poppy Seed Crackers (page 172), I think you'll agree. Plus, they're both fun and easy to make for pennies!

TIME REQUIRED: *about 15 minutes active; 45 minutes passive*
YIELD: *12 ounces*

2 cups whole-wheat flour, plus more as needed

¼ cup olive oil

1 teaspoon kosher salt

½ teaspoon baking powder

3 tablespoons sesame seeds

Salt for topping (use flaky *fleur de sel* or other fancy salt if you have some; otherwise, kosher is fine)

Put the 2 cups flour, ¾ cup cool water, the oil, kosher salt, and baking powder in a food processor and process until the mixture forms a ball, 2 to 3 minutes. Remove from the processor, cover with a towel to prevent drying, and let the dough rest at room temperature for at least 30 minutes and up to 2 hours.

Preheat the oven to 400 degrees F. If you have a pizza stone, preheat that as well. If not, a baking sheet will work fine, but there's no need to preheat it.

Divide the dough into two equal portions. On a lightly floured work surface, roll out the dough very thinly and evenly, flipping it over and continuing to roll while adding more flour as needed if the dough sticks. Stop rolling just short of ⅛ inch thick. Sprinkle the dough lightly with the sesame seeds and flaky salt and continue to roll just to embed the salt and seeds into the dough. Cut into strips about 2 inches wide and poke the strips evenly in several places with the tines of a

continued...

fork. Using both hands, pick up either end of each strip carefully and lay it down on the pizza stone. Bake until the crackers begin to brown and become crisp, keeping in mind that they will continue to crisp up as they cool. If they don't crisp up properly after they cool slightly, you can put them back in the oven for a few minutes. Total baking time takes about 10 minutes on a stone and 15 minutes on a baking sheet. You will need to bake in two or three batches.

Let the crackers cool completely and break them into irregular shards of the desired size and shape. Store in an airtight container. They will stay crisp for at least 2 weeks at room temperature.

CORNMEAL, PARMESAN, AND POPPY SEED CRACKERS

You won't believe how easy it is to make your own crackers and you'll feel great knowing that you can pronounce all of the ingredients. Crunchy cornmeal combined with the umami savoriness of Parmesan makes these true crowd-pleasers. They're neutral enough to pair well with cheese, but flavorful enough to stand alone. The dough is sturdy and easy to work with. Feel free to experiment by adding spices, herbs, or different types of cheese.

TIME REQUIRED: *about 15 minutes active; 45 minutes passive excluding butter preparation)*
YIELD: *about 14 ounces*

1 cup unbleached all-purpose flour, plus more as needed

1 cup cornmeal

½ cup lightly packed finely grated Parmesan cheese

3 tablespoons Cultured Butter (page 121) or store-bought butter, softened

¾ teaspoon kosher salt

2 tablespoons poppy seeds

Salt for topping (use flaky *fleur de sel* or other fancy salt if you have some; otherwise, kosher is fine)

Put the 1 cup flour, cornmeal, ¾ cup cool water, the cheese, butter, and kosher salt in a food processor and process until the mixture forms a ball, 2 to 3 minutes. Remove from the processor, cover with a towel to prevent drying, and let the dough rest at room temperature for at least 30 minutes and up to 2 hours.

Preheat the oven to 400 degrees F. If you have a pizza stone, preheat that as well. If not, a baking sheet will work fine, but there's no need to preheat it.

Divide the dough into two equal portions. On a lightly floured work surface, roll out the dough very thinly and evenly, flipping it over and continuing to roll while adding more flour as needed if the dough sticks. Stop rolling just short of ⅛ inch thick. Sprinkle the dough lightly with the poppy seeds and flaky salt and continue to roll just to embed the salt and seeds into the dough. Cut into strips about 2 inches wide and poke the strips evenly in several places with the tines of a fork. Using both hands, pick up either end of each strip carefully and lay it down on

the pizza stone. Bake until the crackers begin to brown and become crisp, keeping in mind that the crackers will continue to crisp up as they cool. If they don't crisp up properly after they cool slightly, you can put them back in the oven for a few minutes. Total baking time takes about 12 minutes on a stone and 15 to 18 minutes on a baking sheet. You will need to bake in two or three batches.

Let the crackers cool completely and break them into irregular shards of the desired size and shape. Store in an airtight container. They will stay crisp for up to 2 weeks at room temperature.

GRANOLA YOUR WAY

There are many advantages to making your own granola. You'll use less pack-aging, you'll save money, and you can completely customize it to your taste and health needs. You'll never go back to store-bought. The basic ingredients in gra-nola include grain flakes, dried fruit, nuts and seeds, sweetener, and fat, such as butter or vegetable oil. You can embellish with vanilla, coconut, and spices like cinnamon. What follows is a formula to help you create the granola of your dreams, to enjoy every morning. See page 177 for mix-and-match suggestions.

TIME REQUIRED: *10 minutes active; 25 minutes passive*

YIELD: *2 quarts*

⅓ to ½ cup butter or vegetable oil (as desired)

⅓ to ½ cup sweetener (you will need the lesser amount if using agave syrup or honey)

Vanilla, cinnamon, ginger, or cardamom

4 cups flaked grains, such as oat, kamut, rye

Coconut, wheat germ, nutritional yeast, flax seeds, chia seeds (optional)

2 cups (about 8 ounces) lightly chopped nuts (any proportion)

1 cup chopped dried fruit

Preheat the oven to 350 degrees F.

In a small saucepan over medium-low heat, melt the butter (or, if using oil, warm it) and add the sweetener along with the vanilla, cinnamon, or other spices you're using. If using honey for the sweetener, see the variation.

In a large bowl, combine the flaked grains, coconut or wheat germ, seeds, and nuts. Toss to mix. Pour the warmed butter or oil and sweetener over and toss with a large spoon or spatula until evenly and lightly coated.

continued...

Transfer the mixture to a large baking sheet and spread out evenly in a thin layer. You may need to use two baking sheets. Bake until evenly browned, 20 to 25 minutes. Stop halfway through and stir the ingredients so that they brown evenly. Remove from the oven, add the dried fruit, and toss to combine. Let the granola cool completely on the baking sheet and store at room temperature in an airtight container. It will stay fresh for up to 3 weeks, stored properly. I store mine in mason jars on the counter. It looks nice and keeps the granola fresh and handy.

VARIATION: *If using honey, there's no need to heat the oil first, but you still need to melt the butter (if using). Just whisk the fat together with the vanilla or cinnamon and pour it over the flakes, nuts, and extras, and toss and bake as directed. When you remove the granola from the oven, add the dried fruit, and drizzle the honey over it while still warm, toss to coat, and cool and store as directed.*

Note that honey will produce a sticky granola that clumps together. It's not unpleasant, just more difficult to portion as you can't pour it, and it's difficult to scoop.

Mix-and-Match Guide to Custom Granola

Here's where we play. Mix and match the items below to come up with your own dream granola. You'll want to change it up depending on the season and your spirit of adventure.

SWEETENER OPTIONS (USE ONE)

- Brown sugar
- Maple syrup
- Honey
- Agave syrup

FAT OPTIONS (USE ONE)

- Butter
- Coconut oil
- Vegetable oil
- Olive oil

FLAKY OPTIONS (USE ONE OR MORE)

- Oat flakes
- Kamut flakes
- Triticale flakes
- Spelt flakes
- Rye flakes

NUT AND SEED OPTIONS (USE ONE OR MORE)

- Chopped or sliced almonds
- Chopped pecans
- Chopped walnuts
- Pumpkin seeds
- Sesame seeds
- Sunflower seeds

DRIED FRUIT (UNSULFURED AND CHOPPED EVENLY IS BEST) OPTIONS (USE ONE OR MORE)

- Apples
- Pears
- Peaches
- Plums
- Cranberries
- Currants
- Raisins
- Cherries

WHOLE-GRAIN PORRIDGES

My talented friend Rachel Cole is so devoted to porridge that she's actually written a multipage porridge manifesto. I was intrigued when I heard about it. Then I tasted one version of her porridge and was smitten. Make that ruined. Never again will I be as enamored with my rolled oats, dried fruit, and brown sugar combo. There is a big, beautiful world of grains out there that can be combined in both mathematically and gastronomically significant permutations.

There are a few life-changing aspects to joining Rachel's secret porridge society: Homemade porridge is healthful, incredibly tasty, very easy, super-cheap, and fun!

I wasn't allowed to read the manifesto, but she generously shared with me her basic philosophy of porridge. From that I was able to gather enough information to start to experiment and to pass on some valuable knowledge to you.

First thing: You absolutely need a Crock-Pot or slow cooker. That's what makes the process effortless, good, and fun.

All you do is put your chosen combination of grains in the Crock-Pot with some water before you go to bed, and you'll wake up to something wonderful. No time involved. So instead of trotting off to work with your little packet of bland, instant oatmeal to microwave, you can truly nourish yourself with delicious whole grains, which you can just as easily microwave. Your day cannot fail to go well with a belly full of hot porridge. One batch makes a lot, but you can portion it into perfect grab-on-the-go meals to reheat all week.

Start with the grains: Use any whole grains you want, including steel-cut oats; oat groats; kamut; brown, black, red, or white rice; wheat berries; farro; quinoa; amaranth; even hominy. Use what's local to your area and what you like. Combine them in different proportions to get exciting textural variations.

continued...

I like to start with one base grain, like rice or steel-cut oats, then add a smaller proportion of one very chewy grain, like wheat berries, kamut, or hominy. Then I add an even smaller proportion of something fluffy and small, like quinoa or amaranth. Proportions are variable and fairly foolproof. If you like a thick porridge, use approximately 1 cup grains to 3 cups water. For a thinner porridge, use approximately 1 cup grains to 4 cups water. I recommend starting with more water until you see how different grains perform in your particular Crock-Pot. Look at the recipes on page 182 to get an idea for proportions. Start by cooking on low. It should be sufficient for most grains.

If you want to get really adventurous (and more nutritious), add a few tablespoons of legumes like adzuki beans, lentils, or mung beans; or use some raw diced winter squash or sweet potatoes. You can also add flax seeds or chia seeds at this point.

Sometimes I make savory porridges and sometimes sweet. Sweet porridges benefit from cinnamon or other sweet spices added during the cooking and they'll smell so delicious they'll help you get out of bed!

"When your alarm clock goes off and you're not excited
to get out of bed, your breakfast isn't delicious enough."
—Rachel Cole

I hope that some day Rachel publishes her porridge manifesto. But until then, we'll have to make do with our own creativity. After you figure out your grain combo, think about what to add afterward: sweeteners (if desired), liquids or dairy additions, crunchy additions, and stir-ins. Mix and match from the lists on page 183 and have fun creating your own.

TWO PORRIDGE RECIPES

SWEET

TIME REQUIRED: *5 minutes active; 7 to 9 hours passive*
YIELD: *4 to 6 servings*

4½ cups water

⅓ cup brown rice

⅓ cup Bhutanese red rice

⅓ cup wheat berries

¼ cup quinoa

2 teaspoons ground cinnamon

Brown sugar for serving

Milk for serving

Strawberries, sliced, for serving

Combine the water, brown and red rice, wheat berries, quinoa, and cinnamon in a Crock-Pot and cook overnight (or for 7 to 9 hours) on low. Serve with brown sugar, milk, and strawberries.

SAVORY

TIME REQUIRED: *5 minutes active; 7 to 9 hours passive*
YIELD: *4 to 6 servings*

6 cups water

1 cup steel-cut oats

½ cup hominy, soaked for at least 8 hours and then chopped coarsely

¼ cup amaranth

Poached egg for serving

Cheddar cheese for serving

Simple Tomato Salsa (page 72) for serving

Combine the water, oats, hominy, and amaranth in a Crock-Pot and cook overnight (or for 7 to 9 hours) on low. Serve with a poached egg, Cheddar cheese, and Salsa.

Mix-and-Match Guide to Porridge Add-ins

Your homemade porridge is endlessly customizable. For a traditional sweetened breakfast porridge, choose desired add-ons from each category below and enjoy. A savory porridge might include fresh cheese, yogurt, sausage, eggs, or anything else you can think of.

SWEETENERS

- Honey

- Maple syrup

- Plum-Verbena Jam (page 50) or other homemade or store-bought jam

- Brown sugar

- Agave syrup

LIQUIDS AND DAIRY ADDITIONS

- Yogurt (page 98)

- Soy milk

- Almond Milk (page 221)

- Cow or goat milk

- Coconut milk

- Fresh Whole-Milk Soft Cheese (page 106)

- Crème Fraîche (page 116)

CRUNCHY ADDITIONS

- Granola Your Way (page 175)

- Toasted nuts or seeds

STIR-INS

- Roasted Peanut Butter (page 68) or Raw Almond Butter (page 63)

- Fresh fruit

- Dried fruit

- Coconut flakes

CHAPTER FIVE

PICKLES AND FERMENTS

ALMOST EVERY HUMAN CULTURE incorporates a variety of pickled or fermented vegetables into meals. Traditionally used as a way to preserve foods, extend shelf life, and add flavor, pickled and live-culture foods can add interest, texture, and excitement to the simplest meals. Examples of common fermented foods include cheese, kimchi, salami, sourdough bread, and wine. Wild fermented foods are made by adding salt to vegetables to inhibit spoilage while the vegetables are left out at room temperature to allow the wild yeasts and bacteria in the environment to colonize the food. These wild organisms multiply rapidly as they work to preserve the foods. They also contain beneficial organisms that are thought to improve digestion and general well-being, and they taste great. Pickles are preserved through the use of vinegar and salt and can be made with a wide variety of vegetables. Different kinds of pickles abound throughout the world, including common pickled cucumbers, Japanese pickled radish, and Indian mango pickle.

This chapter includes a variety of pickles and wild fermented vegetables along with suggestions for using them in or alongside other recipes in the chapter. Small-batch pickling and fermenting is the focus, but readers who wish to preserve larger quantities for shelf-stable storage can adapt the recipes by using the processing chart in any good canning book (see Sources, page 229).

SIMPLE WILD SAUERKRAUT

Sauerkraut is often thought of as a German dish, but the first sauerkraut was probably created in China. Before refrigeration, it was a great way to preserve fresh vegetables for traveling workers and armies. The technique is easy and lends itself to a variety of different vegetables. Once you've made this a few times, you'll want to experiment with different vegetables and embellishments. On the 'kraut continuum, on one end, there's just cabbage and salt. On the other end, you'll see many other types of vegetables (and sometimes fruits), including whole cabbages, turnips, or beets (I've even seen people ferment mashed potatoes). In the middle, you have something like this: mostly cabbage, a few different vegetables to add interest, and some whole spices or aromatics. I like to play with garlic, ginger, or other types of whole spices. In the winter, when the kale and daikon radish are at their best, I will add them instead of carrots and turnips. Think of this as a nice basic 'kraut to help you build skills and confidence.

TIME REQUIRED: *15 minutes active; 5 to 10 days passive*
YIELD: *1 quart*

1 medium head green cabbage (about 1½ pounds), quartered, cored, and sliced as thinly as possible

2 to 3 carrots, grated on the large holes of a box grater

3 to 4 red turnips, grated on the large holes of a box grater

1 tablespoon plus 1 teaspoon kosher salt

¼ teaspoon mustard seeds or fennel seeds, lightly crushed

Put all the vegetables in a large bowl along with the salt and mustard seeds. With clean hands, toss and squeeze the vegetables until they start to soften and release their liquid (about 5 minutes). Pack them tightly into a 1-quart, wide-mouthed, glass mason jar, pushing down on them with a wooden spoon or your fingertips with as much force as you can until the level of liquid rises above the vegetables. Put a smaller jar inside the glass jar and push down on it to keep the vegetables submerged. Cover with a clean towel and secure with a rubber band. This is to allow the 'kraut to breathe while keeping bugs out.

Leave out at room temperature for about 5 days. Check once daily to be sure the vegetables stay submerged, pushing down on them if needed. If you see a foamy scum, simply skim it off. Taste daily, starting on the third day. The sauerkraut is ready when it tastes good to you. This could be anywhere from 3 to 10 days. When it's to your liking, fasten the lid and transfer it to the refrigerator. Sauer-kraut will last for months in the refrigerator. It doesn't really go bad, but older 'kraut can become unpalatably soft, almost mushy. Some people like to cook it when it gets to that point—in a bean soup or with sausages and potatoes.

Sarma: Serbian Stuffed Cabbage Rolls with Sauerkraut

This is pretty much the version my mother made when I was growing up, but there was no recipe, so my sister and I re-created this one from our flavor memories. Even though my mother didn't, I've added Simple Wild Sauerkraut because I happen to love it, and I know many people bake their stuffed cabbage with sauerkraut. For a real Balkan bacchanal, kick off dinner with an appetizer of Ajvar (page 74) and Easy Yogurt Cheese (page 99) served with Whole-Wheat Sesame Crackers (page 169) or crostini. This recipe nicely illustrates how, with very little money, you can feed a lot of people gorgeous, filling, nutritious food.

TIME REQUIRED: *45 minutes active; about 2 hours passive (excluding sauerkraut and ketchup preparation)*
YIELD: *6 to 8 servings*

CABBAGE ROLLS

1 large head green cabbage (2 to 2½ pounds, see Note, facing page)

1½ pounds ground beef (local pasture-raised if possible)

½ cup uncooked, long-grain white rice

½ small yellow onion, very finely chopped

1 large egg, beaten

1¼ teaspoons salt

¼ teaspoon freshly ground black pepper

SAUCE

2 tablespoons olive oil

½ small yellow onion, diced (about ½ cup)

One 28-ounce can crushed tomatoes

Salt

3 to 6 tablespoons Real Ketchup (page 37) or store-bought ketchup (see Tip, facing page)

3 cups Simple Wild Sauerkraut (page 186)

To make the rolls: Bring about 3 inches of salted water to a boil in a large pot. Core the cabbage, leaving it whole, and put it in the pot, covered. Cook until the leaves are pliable, but still retain their structure, about 12 minutes, turning once. Remove and drain until cool enough to handle. Reserve the cabbage water.

In a large bowl, mix together the beef, rice, onion, egg, salt, and pepper just until blended.

To make the sauce: In a medium saucepan, warm the oil. Add the onion and sauté until soft. Add the tomatoes and a pinch of salt, stir, and bring to a simmer. Simmer while you stuff the rolls, until the sauce thickens and the flavors are blended, about 15 minutes. Add the ketchup, gradually, to taste.

Stuff the rolls. Carefully peel the large leaves from the poached cabbage. Using a sharp paring knife, gently trim some of the thick vein from the back of the larger leaves. This will make them easier to roll. Lay the leaves out on a flat surface. Spoon about 3 tablespoons of the beef mixture into each leaf, depending on the size of the cabbage leaves. Roll up each leaf lengthwise and tuck the ends in with your fingers to make little packets. If the leaves won't hold together, use a toothpick to secure them at the seam. You should have about 15 rolls.

Select a Dutch oven large enough to contain all the rolls and the sauerkraut. Spread the sauerkraut out on the bottom of the Dutch oven, covering it. Lay the rolls on top of the sauerkraut. You can make multiple layers.

Pour about 2 cups of the cabbage water into the tomato sauce and stir. If you don't have enough cabbage water, make up the difference with tap water. Pour the sauce over the rolls and bring the whole pot to a simmer over medium-high heat.

Preheat the oven to 350 degrees F.

Lower the heat under the Dutch oven to medium-low and simmer, partially covered, until the sauce begins to cling to the cabbage leaves, about 20 minutes. Cover completely, transfer the pot to the oven, and cook until the sauce thickens, the cabbage is soft, and the rolls are very hot inside, 1½ hours. Serve hot with sauce spooned over. This one-dish meal has all the components you need, but you may want to serve it with a salad or a cooked vegetable and bread to scoop up the sauce.

NOTE: *Some traditional cabbage-roll recipes used cabbage leaves from whole heads of cabbage fermented in giant crocks and kept through the winter. I'm sure the step of boiling the cabbage was developed as a short-cut method of softening the leaves, as if they'd been fermented. But there is no substitute for the taste. If I ever get one of those big fermenting crocks, I plan to try it sometime.*

✓TIP: *If using store-bought ketchup, be careful not to add too much as it's sweeter than Real Ketchup.*

SPICY KIMCHI

I adapted this recipe from one I learned in a workshop at the Asian Culinary Forum in San Francisco with Huynjoo Albrecht, of CookingKorean.com. If you've only had commercial kimchi, which is sometimes overly salty and very spicy while lacking dimension, you'll be surprised at the complexity of this version. Lightly fermented and spicy, to be sure, the nuances of the individual components come through in layers. If you're worried about making it too spicy, start with less red pepper the first time you make it and see how you like it. It's wonderful with Spicy Soft Tofu Soup (page 194), served alongside brown rice and fish, or tossed into a seasonal grain salad (see page 93).

If you have access to a Korean market, buy the medium ground Korean red pepper powder for kimchi, which usually comes in a one-pound plastic bag. Make sure that it doesn't have salt or other additives. Or see Sources (page 227). You can also experiment with a milder cayenne pepper; a mild ground red chile, such as New Mexico; or Aleppo pepper, a mild red pepper used in Middle Eastern cooking that has a nice fruity flavor and a similar heat level to Korean pepper. This recipe is written for kosher salt. If you're using a finer-grained sea salt, you will need to use about 25 percent less.

TIME REQUIRED: *45 minutes active; 9 hours plus 3 days passive*

YIELD: *1 quart*

2½ cups plus 1 tablespoon kosher salt

1 head Napa cabbage, untrimmed (about 2½ pounds)

½ pound daikon radish, peeled and grated on the large holes of a box grater

2 green onions, finely chopped (white and green parts)

¼ cup mild ground Korean red pepper powder (see head note)

2 garlic cloves, finely chopped

One 1-inch piece fresh ginger, peeled and finely chopped

1 tablespoon soy sauce

1 tablespoon sugar

1½ teaspoons sesame oil

1 teaspoon toasted white sesame seeds

continued...

Dissolve 1¼ cups of the salt in 2 quarts of water. Test the proper amount of salt by gently placing an egg in the water. If it floats, the salt solution is perfect. If it sinks, add a little more salt.

Peel just the outer leaves from the cabbage and discard or compost them. Then, leaving it untrimmed, quarter it lengthwise through the root end, so the root holds each quarter together. Sprinkle 1¼ cups more salt between the cabbage leaves. Starting from the outer layer, lift each leaf and sprinkle salt on it, dividing the salt evenly, so that each layer of cabbage is salted. Put the cabbage in the salted water and place a weighted plate on top to keep it fully submerged.

Toss the grated radish in the remaining 1 tablespoon salt and let it drain in a colander while the cabbage soaks in its water bath.

The cabbage should soak until the heavy white parts of the cabbage closest to the root end are pliable but not mushy. Try bending one or two leaves. If they break, the cabbage hasn't soaked long enough. It should take 3 or 4 hours, depending on the room's temperature. In the end, the cabbage should offer a little resistance but not break.

Remove the cabbage from the salted water and rinse it thoroughly under running water several times (this is important or your kimchi will be too salty). Squeeze lightly and place the cabbage quarters, root-side up, in a colander to drain. Drain for 1 hour. Rinse the radish, squeeze out the excess moisture, and continue to drain it.

Meanwhile, in a large bowl, combine the onions, red pepper powder, garlic, ginger, soy sauce, sugar, sesame oil, and sesame seeds.

Squeeze the drained cabbage to remove as much water as possible. Slice the cabbage crosswise into pieces 1 to 1½ inches wide. Add them to the bowl with the seasonings. Add the drained daikon and toss to coat thoroughly.

Transfer the kimchi and its juices to a 1-quart, wide-mouth mason jar and push it down with a wooden spoon. Fasten the lid and let it sit undisturbed at room temperature for 4 to 5 hours, depending on the warmth of the room. Refrigerate for 2 to 3 days to let the flavors develop before eating. It should taste balanced, but spicy and lightly fermented. It keeps, refrigerated, for several months.

Spicy Soft Tofu Soup with Kimchi

Inspired by the soft tofu soups served in Korean restaurants, but using a quick and flavorful Japanese broth, this soup is an easy way to incorporate your homemade Spicy Kimchi into a meal. This dish is healthful, light, and low in calories. It's perfect for those feeling a little under the weather or simply trying to eat lightly. The dashi broth that you'll make in this recipe is the mother broth of Japanese cooking and has multiple uses in a resourceful kitchen. Use it to simmer vegetables or seafood for a light dinner; add miso, tofu, and green onions to make miso soup; or simmer noodles and fish together with greens for a quick dinner. See Sources on page 226 for information on locating any hard-to-find ingredients.

TIME REQUIRED: *15 minutes active; 25 minutes passive (excluding kimchi preparation)*

YIELD: *4 servings*

Two 5-by-3-inch pieces kombu

1 cup bonito flakes

1 large shallot, thinly sliced

2 garlic cloves, finely chopped

1 tablespoon Korean red pepper powder or about ½ teaspoon cayenne pepper (depending on its heat level and your taste)

Salt

1 turnip, peeled, sliced, and julienned

1 carrot, peeled, sliced, and julienned

2 ounces fresh mushrooms, such as shiitake or cremini, sliced

½ ounce dried mushrooms, such as shiitake or wood ear, rehydrated and sliced thinly

¼ ounce wakame seaweed

One 14-ounce package organic soft tofu, cut into 1-inch pieces

Thinly sliced green onions (green and white parts) for garnish

Toasted sesame oil for drizzling

Spicy Kimchi (page 191) for garnish

continued...

In a large saucepan over medium heat, bring 2 quarts of water and the kombu to a boil. Turn off the heat and add the bonito flakes. Don't stir. Let the broth sit, undisturbed, until the bonito flakes sink to the bottom, about 5 minutes. Strain the broth into a bowl through a very fine strainer, or through a regular strainer lined with a coffee filter.

Rinse the saucepan and return the broth to it. Bring the broth to a boil and add the shallot, garlic, red pepper powder, and a little salt and simmer for 10 minutes. Taste and correct the salt. Add the turnip, carrot, mushrooms, and seaweed and simmer until the vegetables are crisp-tender, about 10 minutes. Add the tofu and simmer for another few minutes, to warm it through.

Ladle the soup into deep bowls and garnish each serving with green onions, a drizzle of sesame oil, and kimchi.

LACTO-FERMENTED
BABY BEETS

The process used here is similar to the one used for Simple Wild Sauerkraut (page 186), Wild Salvadoran Curtido (page 198), and Spicy Kimchi (page 191). Rather than vinegar, all of these vegetables are preserved with the help of salt, while the lactic acid bacteria that are naturally present starts the work of fermenting the vegetables. In the case of these beets, I've used whey obtained from draining yogurt to introduce the lactic acid directly. Many people use this method in place of brining with salt, but I like salt, so I use both. The lactic acid feeds on the sugar in the beets, introducing a gentle sourness. These beets will remain quite crisp after fermentation. Don't discard the brine after finishing your beets. It's a wonderful tonic drink that some people swear by as a liver cleanser. It's very similar to beet kvass, which is made from fermented beets. You can also use it to make vinaigrette.

TIME REQUIRED: *10 to 15 minutes active; 8 to 10 days passive*
YIELD: *1 quart*

1 ½ pounds baby beets (about 25 to 30)

⅛ teaspoon mustard seeds

2 cups non-chlorinated water (see Note)

¼ cup whey from drained chese (see page 106)

1 tablespoon kosher salt

Scrub the beets and peel them if you wish (sometimes I just cut off the rough parts with a paring knife). Put them in a clean, 1-quart mason jar with the mustard seeds. Combine the water and whey in a small bowl. Add the salt and stir to dissolve.

Pour the water and whey over the beets to submerge. Cover the jar with a tea towel and fasten with a rubber band. Leave it out at room temperature for about 10 days, depending on the warmth of the weather. Start testing after 6 days by tasting a slice of one of the beets. When they are done, they will remain crisp all the way through but a slight sourness will overtake the beet's natural earthiness and they will no longer taste raw. Seal the jar and refrigerate them in their brine at this point. They will last for several months.

NOTE: *Some municipalities chlorinate the water. If this is true of your area, use bottled water, as chlorine can inhibit the fermentation process.*

WILD SALVADORAN CURTIDO

If you've ever eaten a pupusa *in a Salvadoran restaurant, you've probably had the tangy cabbage salad called* curtido *that is usually served alongside them. Inhabiting the same culinary niche as Spicy Kimchi (page 191) or Simple Wild Sauerkraut (page 186),* curtido *is the perfect companion to any rich, heavy, or meaty dish. In addition to* pupusas, *I've enjoyed it on both fish and meat tacos, with quesadillas, on top of simply cooked beans with tortillas, or stirred into a bean soup, posole, or other Latin American–inspired soup. Using the same technique as Simple Wild Sauerkraut and with a very different flavor profile,* curtido *is so simple to make and so versatile, you might find it becoming a staple in your kitchen. For my taste, I like a lighter ferment than for sauerkraut so I tend to only let my* curtido *ferment for three to five days. You'll want to taste it every day starting on day two and decide how you like it.*

TIME REQUIRED: *15 minutes active; 3 to 5 days passive*
YIELD: *1 quart*

1 medium head green cabbage (about 1½ pounds), quartered, cored, and sliced as thinly as possible

½ small onion, sliced thinly

2 to 3 carrots, peeled and grated on the large holes of a box grater

1 tablespoon plus 1 teaspoon kosher salt

2 jalapeños, cut in quarters lengthwise, seeded and sliced thinly

½ teaspoon dried Mexican oregano, crushed

Put the cabbage, onion, and carrots in a large bowl. Add the salt and, with clean hands, toss and squeeze the vegetables until they start to soften and release their liquid (about 5 minutes). Add the jalapeños and oregano and toss to distribute. Pack the mixture tightly into a 1-quart, wide-mouthed, glass Mason jar, pushing down on the vegetables with a wooden spoon or your fingertips with as much force as you can until the level of liquid rises above the vegetables. Put a smaller jar inside the glass jar to keep the vegetables submerged. Cover with a clean tea towel and secure with a rubber band. The *curtido* needs to breathe.

Leave out at room temperature for about 3 to 5 days. Check once daily to be sure the vegetables stay submerged, pushing down on them if needed. If you see a frothy residue on the surface, simply skim it off. Taste daily starting on the second day. The *curtido* is ready when it tastes good to you. When it's to your liking, fasten the lid and transfer it to the refrigerator. It will last for months in the refrigerator. It doesn't really go bad but will soften over time.

BREAD AND BUTTER PICKLES

Sweet and a little spicy, these classics are great on sandwiches and paired with creamy cheeses. I think they go surprisingly well with Southeast Asian–inspired dishes like grilled chicken with Spicy Southeast Asian Peanut Sauce (page 69), and they're perfect chopped up in egg, potato, or chicken salad.

TIME REQUIRED: *15 minutes active; 3 days passive*
YIELD: *1 pint*

About ¾ pound medium pickling or Persian cucumbers (4 to 5), peeled and sliced into ¼-inch slices

¾ cup distilled white vinegar

½ cup sugar

½ teaspoon kosher salt

½ teaspoon mustard seeds

¼ teaspoon ground turmeric

Pinch of celery seeds

Pinch of red pepper flakes

Sterilize a 1-pint mason jar and lid with boiling water (see page 50). Drain them and air-dry. Pack the cucumber slices into the jar as tightly as they will go.

In a small saucepan over medium heat, bring ¼ cup water, the vinegar, sugar, salt, mustard seeds, turmeric, celery seeds, and red pepper flakes to a boil. Stir to dissolve the sugar. Lower the heat and let them simmer for 5 minutes. Pour the hot liquid over the cucumbers, fasten the lid, and refrigerate.

Let them sit for 3 days to allow the flavors to develop. They should taste crisp and sweetly sour. They will keep, refrigerated, for several weeks.

ITALIAN TABLE PICKLES

Also called giardiniera, these are the pickled vegetables found in many an Italian antipasti. They're great for your Thanksgiving relish, with sandwiches, or alongside any rich, heavy, or meaty meal. You can use a variety of vegetables, depending on the season: bell peppers, broccoli, cauliflower, onion, carrot, green beans, radishes, fennel—whatever strikes your fancy and is in season. You can make them spicier by adding more red pepper. Whichever vegetables you use, a good rule of thumb is to allow approximately one pound of cut-up vegetables per quart jar. The rough quantities given below add up to about one pound.

TIME REQUIRED: *15 minutes active; 3 days passive*
YIELD: *1 quart*

About ¼ head broccoli, cut into florets

About ¼ head cauliflower, cut into florets

About ¼ red onion, sliced into ½-inch pieces

1 large carrot, cut into bite-sized chunks

3 garlic cloves, sliced

3 sprigs fresh dill

1 cup distilled white vinegar

1 teaspoon sugar

1 teaspoon kosher salt

¼ teaspoon red pepper flakes

¼ teaspoon fennel seeds

¼ teaspoon peppercorns

⅛ teaspoon yellow mustard seeds

Pinch of celery seeds

2 dried bay leaves

Sterilize a 1-quart mason jar and lid with boiling water (see page 50). Drain them and air-dry. Pack the broccoli, cauliflower, onion, carrot, garlic, and dill into the jar. Use a chopstick to distribute the dill and garlic evenly.

In a small saucepan, bring 1 cup water, the vinegar, sugar, salt, and spices to a boil. Stir to dissolve the sugar and salt. Pour the hot brine over the vegetables, fasten the lid, and refrigerate. Let it sit for 3 days or so to let the flavors blend. The pickles will taste crisp and vinegary with a nice balance of salt. They will keep, refrigerated, for several weeks.

PICKLED KOHLRABI AND TURNIPS WITH CARDAMOM

These easy refrigerator pickles are wonderfully versatile. Enjoy them as a snack or on sandwiches or serve them with Simple Dal (facing page) drizzled with homemade Yogurt (page 98). Kohlrabi is a crisp, slightly sweet and spicy brassica vegetable that I believe is underutilized and underappreciated in American kitchens. Like turnips, it can be cooked, but I enjoy it raw or pickled best.

TIME REQUIRED: *30 minutes active; 3 days passive*
YIELD: *1 quart*

About ¾ pound turnips

About ¾ pound kohlrabi

1⅓ cups distilled white vinegar

2 garlic cloves, peeled and left whole

2 teaspoons sugar

2 teaspoons kosher salt

4 green cardamom pods, lightly crushed

6 whole peppercorns

½ teaspoon mustard seeds, lightly crushed

½ teaspoon ground turmeric

Peel the turnips and kohlrabi and cut them into quarters. Cut the quarters into ¼-inch wedges (after trimming, the yield is about 1 pound total).

Sterilize a 1-quart, wide-mouth mason jar and lid with boiling water (see page 50). Drain them and air-dry.

In a nonreactive, heavy, medium saucepan, combine ⅔ cup water, the vinegar, garlic, sugar, salt, cardamom, peppercorns, mustard seeds, and turmeric. Bring to a boil, lower the heat to a simmer, and cook for 10 to 15 minutes.

Pack the cut vegetables into the mason jar and pour the hot vinegar and spice mixture over them. Fasten the lid and refrigerate immediately. Refrigerate the pickles for 3 days before enjoying to allow the flavors to blend. The pickles will be crisp and infused with spices. They will keep, refrigerated, for several weeks.

SIMPLE DAL

This dish perfectly illustrates how to eat simply, cheaply, and healthfully by using the building blocks in this book to make a complete meal. Cook some brown rice and make this dish in thirty minutes or so with nothing more than red lentils and a few simple spices. Accompany it with a side of sautéed greens, Pickled Kohlrabi and Turnips with Cardamom (facing page), homemade Yogurt (page 98) or Easy Yogurt Cheese (page 99), Ajvar (page 74), and homemade bread or even Flour Tortillas (page 136), and you have a very nice meal that doesn't pretend to be authentic to any one culture but whose flavors and textures go together beautifully. I encourage you to mix and match this book's building blocks in whatever ways interest you. Of course you've invested time up front on some of the accompaniments, but it's like time in the bank later.

TIME REQUIRED: *about 30 minutes
(excluding accompaniment preparation)*
YIELD: *4 servings*

1 cup split red lentils	2 small, dried red chiles
½ teaspoon ground turmeric	½ teaspoon cumin seeds
Salt	¼ teaspoon mustard seeds
2 tablespoons vegetable oil	2 garlic cloves, finely chopped
½ yellow or red onion, thinly sliced	Freshly ground black pepper

Rinse the lentils and put them in a medium saucepan with 4 cups water, the turmeric, and a few pinches of salt. Bring to a boil, lower the heat to a bare simmer, and cover partially. Cook until the lentils are soft and resemble a thick, textured porridge, stirring occasionally and watching so it doesn't boil over or scorch, 15 to 20 minutes.

In a heavy, medium skillet over medium-high heat, warm the oil. Add the onion and cook, stirring, until it begins to brown, about 5 minutes. Add the chiles, cumin, and mustard seeds and cook, stirring, for about 1 minute, until the seeds start to pop. Add the garlic and cook, stirring, for 30 seconds. Stir this mixture into the lentils and cover. Let them sit for 5 minutes or so to blend the flavors. Season with salt and pepper. Serve with the accompaniments suggested in the head note.

SPICY PICKLED GREEN BEANS

These spicy, garden-fresh beans are wonderful as part of a relish tray, served alongside sandwiches, tucked into a Bloody Mary, or tossed into Potato Salad with Spicy Pickled Green Beans and Hard-Cooked Eggs (facing page).

TIME REQUIRED: *15 minutes active; 3 days passive*
YIELD: *1 quart*

1 pound green beans, stems snapped off and left whole

2 fresh mild red chiles (such as Fresno), quartered lengthwise and seeded

2 garlic cloves, thinly sliced

3 or 4 sprigs fresh dill

1⅓ cups distilled white vinegar

1 tablespoon sugar

2 teaspoons kosher salt

1 teaspoon yellow mustard seeds

Sterilize a 1-quart mason jar and its lid with boiling water (see page 50). Drain them and air-dry.

Pack the green beans, chiles, garlic, and dill into the jar in alternating layers, distributing them evenly.

In a small saucepan over medium heat, bring ⅔ cup water, the vinegar, sugar, salt, and mustard seeds to a boil. Stir to dissolve the sugar and let the mixture boil for 5 minutes. Pour the hot liquid over the green beans, fasten the lid, and refrigerate. Let it sit for 3 days to blend the flavors. The beans will remain crisp, with the flavors of the spices evident. The pickled green beans will keep, refrigerated, for several weeks.

Potato Salad with Spicy Pickled Green Beans and Hard-Cooked Eggs

This salad has a down-home uncomplicated taste, like a mid-day Sunday farmhouse supper—roasted chicken, biscuits, potato salad, and iced tea, all laid out on a checkered tablecloth. I really like the combination of tart, spicy green beans; creamy potatoes; and hard-cooked eggs. You don't even have to make a dressing. Just toss with olive oil and pickle juice from the Spicy Pickled Green Beans (facing page). If you want to make this salad but don't have any pickles on hand, replace the pickled green beans with fresh steamed green beans and make Basic Best-Ever Vinaigrette (page 84) to dress the salad.

TIME REQUIRED: *20 minutes active; 20 minutes passive (excluding pickle preparation)*
YIELD: *6 to 8 servings*

4 large eggs

1½ pounds young fingerling or Yukon gold potatoes

1 small red onion, thinly sliced

1 bunch radishes (about 6), halved and thinly sliced

1 celery rib, cut in half lengthwise and thinly sliced on the diagonal

1½ cups Spicy Pickled Green Beans (facing page), cut into 1-inch lengths, juices reserved

¼ cup chopped fresh flat-leaf parsley

1 tablespoon snipped fresh chives

1 tablespoon chopped fresh dill

¼ cup olive oil

Salt

Freshly ground black pepper

Put the eggs in a small saucepan and cover with cold water. Bring to a boil over medium-high heat. Turn off the heat, cover, and leave the eggs undisturbed for 12 minutes (15 minutes if the eggs are very large). Drain the eggs and run cold water over them. Let them sit in the cold water until you are ready to peel them.

continued...

Meanwhile, wash the potatoes, leaving them unpeeled. In a vegetable steamer over medium-high heat, steam them until tender, about 15 minutes. Remove them from the steamer and let cool slightly.

Cut the potatoes into bite-sized pieces and put them in a large salad bowl. Add the onion, radishes, celery, green beans, and herbs. Peel the eggs and cut them into ½-inch pieces. Add them to the bowl. Toss and add the oil, season with salt and pepper, and add pickle juice to taste. Serve immediately, or within 2 hours at room temperature. This salad tastes best if it's consumed the day it is made and never refrigerated. If you must make it ahead, it will keep, refrigerated, for up to 5 days. Remove from the refrigerator 30 minutes before serving and taste and adjust the salt and pepper.

GARLICKY CUCUMBER PICKLE RELISH

Pounding the garlic helps to distribute its flavor fully throughout this relish. I like a chunky relish like this to spoon over beans or Black-Eyed Peas with Stewed Okra and Tomatoes (page 210). It also works as a fresh salsa on grilled chicken or fish. If you like a finer-textured relish, you can grate the cucumbers instead of dicing them, but you'll need to use a few more to fill your pint.

TIME REQUIRED: *15 minutes active; 20 minutes plus 3 days passive*
YIELD: *1 pint*

1 pound pickling or Persian cucumbers (about 6), peeled

1 teaspoon kosher salt

¾ cup distilled white vinegar

1 teaspoon sugar

1 garlic clove, peeled and left whole

1 small, fresh mild red chile (such as a Fresno), seeded and quartered, then sliced thinly

1 teaspoon chopped fresh dill

Sterilize a 1-pint mason jar and its lid with boiling water (see page 50). Drain them and air-dry.

Cut the cucumbers into quarters lengthwise and scrape out the seeds. Cut each quarter lengthwise in half and then dice it into ¼-inch pieces. If using plump pickling cucumbers, you will need to cut them one more time lengthwise to get a ¼-inch dice. Put the cucumbers in a strainer and sprinkle ½ teaspoon of the salt over them. Toss with your hands to distribute, and let the cucumbers drain for about 30 minutes. Squeeze and massage the cucumbers with your hands once or twice during this time to help them release their liquid.

In a small saucepan over medium heat, bring ¼ cup water, the vinegar, sugar, and remaining ½ teaspoon salt to a boil. Boil for 5 minutes.

Pound the garlic to a paste with a pinch of salt in a mortar and pestle.

Remove the vinegar mixture from the heat and stir in the garlic.

Pack the drained cucumbers, the chile, and dill into the mason jar. Pour the hot vinegar mixture over them and fasten the lid. Refrigerate for 3 days to blend the flavors. The relish will remain crisp with the flavor of garlic and spices permeating the cucumbers. It will keep, refrigerated, for up to 2 weeks.

Black-Eyed Peas with Stewed Okra and Tomatoes with Garlicky Cucumber Pickle Relish

Black-eyed peas are so rich, it's nice to have a little something vinegary and spicy alongside them. For this reason, I always serve this dish with a spoonful of Garlicky Cucumber Pickle Relish. If you've spent much time dining in the South, you will be reminded of the bottles of chile-infused vinegar that are often available for diners to shake over rich, pork-infused greens or red beans and rice. This dish is great on its own, but it becomes a balanced meal when served over rice.

TIME REQUIRED: *30 minutes active; about 1 hour passive (excluding relish preparation)*
YIELD: *6 to 8 servings*

6 tablespoons vegetable oil for high-heat cooking

1 yellow onion, diced

1 celery rib, diced

2 garlic cloves, finely chopped

1 pound dried black-eyed peas, rinsed and drained (see Tip, facing page)

Salt

1 pound fresh okra (choose small pods if available), left whole (see Note, facing page)

Freshly ground black pepper

1 pound fresh Roma tomatoes, cut into ½-inch dice

½ teaspoon smoked paprika

Garlicky Cucumber Pickle Relish (page 208) for serving

In a large soup pot over medium heat, warm 3 tablespoons of the oil. Add half of the diced onion, the celery, and the garlic. Cook, stirring occasionally, until soft and fragrant, about 10 minutes. Add the peas and water to cover by 1 inch. Turn up the heat and bring to a boil. Reduce the heat to medium-low, cover partially, and simmer until the peas are almost tender, about 30 minutes. Stir occasionally to prevent sticking and add a little water, as needed, but don't add too much as this should not be an overly soupy dish. Season with salt. Continue cooking, covered, over low heat until the peas are tender and most of the broth is absorbed, another 15 minutes.

In a large skillet spacious enough to hold all the okra, heat the remaining 3 tablespoons oil over medium-high heat. (I sometimes use a wok because it's large enough to contain all the okra, making it easy to toss.) Add the okra and a little salt and pepper and cook, stirring often, until the okra begins to soften and brown, 8 to 10 minutes. Remove the okra pods from the skillet to a bowl or plate and lower the heat to medium-low. If the okra pods are large (more than 1½ inches long), cut them crosswise on the diagonal into two or three pieces. Add the remaining diced onion, and cook until the onion is fragrant, 7 or 8 minutes. Add the tomatoes and paprika and return the okra to the pan. Cover partially and simmer, stirring occasionally, until the okra is soft and the tomatoes have cooked down, about 10 minutes. Taste and correct the seasoning with salt and pepper.

Serve the stewed okra and tomatoes over the black-eyed peas with the Garlicky Cucumber Pickle Relish on the side.

NOTE: *If you dislike the viscosity of okra, be aware that this characteristic is enhanced by cutting and exposing it to moisture. There are two methods for reducing slime. Buy small okra and cook it whole, never cutting it. Or, if only larger pods are available, cook them over high heat for 10 minutes before cutting and adding them back to the pan with the tomatoes to finish cooking. The initial high heat works to cauterize the okra, preventing excessive slime.*

✓TIP: *You can cook the peas 1 to 3 days ahead and keep them refrigerated until you are ready to cook the okra and tomatoes. The whole dish makes fantastic leftovers.*

CHAPTER SIX

BEVERAGES

WHEN I WAS A KID, sodas were a special once-in-awhile treat. Now, giant bottles of carbonated water, high-fructose corn syrup, chemical additives, and artificial colors are ubiquitous and heavily consumed by both children and adults. As criticism has mounted over soda's stranglehold over school vending machines, the industry has come up with alternative juice and tea drinks that are perceived to be more healthful, but they are still filled with sugar and processed ingredients. However, it's easy and fun to make your own tasty carbonated and non-carbonated drinks. And you'll cut out the chemicals, corn syrup, and excessive packaging. Homemade sodas naturally fermented with yeast are simple enough for kids to make. They'll learn about fermentation and enjoy their homemade sodas as the special treat they were meant to be. Taqueria favorites like horchata (rice milk) and jamaica (hibiscus tea) are great for parties and special occasions. The ancient beverage kombucha, which has become popular commercially over the past few years, is a healthful, raw drink that is naturally fermented and so easy to make at home. Just say "No more!" to over-sweetened bottles of empty calories.

KOMBUCHA

Kombucha is made by fermenting black tea and sugar with a special culture. It is slightly fizzy, a little bit tart, and very refreshing—like a slightly sour apple cider. It contains beneficial bacteria that aid digestion and boost the immune system. The sugar and caffeine are consumed by the culture, so they do not end up in the final product. Many people consider kombucha to be a powerful cure-all. In recent years, several commercial brands have emerged, usually sold in health food stores and specialty groceries. It is much less expensive to make your own. Many of the commercial brands are flavored. You can flavor yours however you like (with crushed fresh berries or other fruit, or with a bit of grated ginger). Do this after the fermentation is complete. I prefer to flavor my kombucha subtly by brewing it with a mixture of black tea and herbal tea. Elderflower tea, which I call for here, makes a light kombucha with a Sauvignon Blanc–like character, but you should experiment on your own once you master the basic method.

TIME REQUIRED: *15 minutes active; 10 to 15 days passive*
YIELD: *1 gallon*

6 black tea bags (I like to use organic oolong)

2 tablespoons loose elderflower tea (or other herbal flower tea), in a tea-infusing sack

1 cup sugar

1 kombucha culture (see Sources, page 226)

Wash a 1-gallon glass container (such as a sun tea jug) in hot soapy water and let it air-dry.

In a large pot, bring 1 gallon water to a boil. Boil for 3 minutes. Meanwhile, put the tea bags and tea sack in another large glass container, such as a 4-cup glass measuring pitcher.

Pour some of the boiling water over the tea bags and let them steep until the water cools completely. Add the sugar to the remaining hot water and stir to dissolve. Let the tea water and the sugar water cool to room temperature.

Put the kombucha culture in the empty glass container. Discard the tea bags and tea sack, and pour the steeped tea and the sugar water into the container with the kombucha culture. Cover the jar with a towel fastened tightly with a rubber band to keep bugs out. (Fruit flies love kombucha.) Do not use a tightly fastened lid, though, as the culture needs to breathe. Place the jar in a cool, dark place (such as a cupboard) for 7 to 10 days. The actual time will depend on your culture and the warmth of the room. Your kombucha will brew faster in hot weather. A film will form on the top of the liquid, which means the culture is working and reproducing. Try not to jostle it while it's brewing because you'll eventually want to use this new culture, so it's best if it stays intact.

Every time you make kombucha, you will produce a new culture. These can be composted or given away to friends. The mother you started with will eventually weaken, so you should always hold back a few "babies" to keep your culture going. When the mother is very dark and rubbery, it should be discarded. After 5 days, begin tasting your kombucha daily. If your container doesn't have a spigot, this can be done with a small spoon. The kombucha is done when it is no longer sweet. It should taste like tart apple cider. Decant it into glass bottles, so there is no headspace and seal tightly with lids, making sure to save a culture to start the process over. Give away or refrigerate extras. Leave in a cool, dark place, undisturbed, for 5 days. This will allow your kombucha to develop a desirable fizziness. Start another batch in your clean, empty container. After 5 days, the bottles of decanted kombucha can be transferred to the refrigerator and enjoyed.

ABOUT HOMEMADE SOFT DRINKS

Making your own soft drinks is simpler than you probably think. It requires nothing more than water, sugar (or other sweeteners), natural flavorings, and yeast to start the fermentation process. Once you get started, you can experiment with different flavors. These recipes call for a special yeast used by home beer brewers, which is easy to find online (see Sources, page 226) or at home-brewer shops. This yeast, like active dry yeast, should be kept refrigerated. Though I prefer glass to plastic, generally speaking, I use plastic 1½-liter bottles from bottled water on the off chance the soda over-ferments and explodes before I can refrigerate it. I've found it's a good way to rotate through my supply of earthquake/disaster water, which shouldn't be kept around for more than a year anyway. Don't let the talk of explosions scare you, though. They are rare and never happen once the soda is refrigerated.

ROOT BEER

The powdered herbs called for are available in the bulk section of well-stocked health food stores and sarsaparilla can be found in home-brewing stores. Read "About Homemade Soft Drinks" (page 216) before getting started.

TIME REQUIRED: *15 minutes active; 2 to 3 days passive*
YIELD: *1½ liters*

2 tablespoons sarsaparilla bark

⅓ to ½ cup sugar

½ teaspoon powdered burdock root

1 teaspoon powdered licorice root

⅛ teaspoon brewing yeast

Pour 1½ liters water into a medium saucepan and add the sarsaparilla. Bring to a boil and simmer for 3 minutes or so to infuse the water. Turn off the heat, and add ⅓ cup sugar, the burdock root, and the licorice root. Stir to dissolve the sugar. Taste, add extra sugar if desired, and then pour through a strainer lined with a coffee filter. Let cool to slightly warmer than body temperature. Stir in the yeast until it dissolves. Pour the strained mixture through a funnel into a plastic bottle, without leaving any head room. If the liquid doesn't fill the bottle, you probably lost some to the strainer. Simply fill to the top with plain warm water. Fasten the cap and let it sit out in a warm place in your kitchen for 24 to 48 hours. When the bottle feels hard to the touch and begins to bulge, refrigerate it. The carbonation should last at least 1 week after opening.

GINGER BEER

Sweet, spicy, and really refreshing, adults really love this. And it makes an excellent cocktail mixer! You'll probably find that the ginger beer ferments faster than the root beer.

TIME REQUIRED: *15 minutes active; 1 to 2 days passive*
YIELD: *1½ liters*

⅓ to ½ cup sugar

1 tablespoon peeled and finely grated fresh ginger

⅛ teaspoon brewing yeast

Pour 1½ liters water into a medium saucepan. Bring to a boil and simmer for 3 minutes or so. Turn off the heat and add ⅓ cup sugar and the ginger. Stir to dissolve the sugar. Taste, add extra sugar if desired, and then pour through a strainer lined with a coffee filter. Let cool to slightly warmer than body temperature. Stir in the yeast until it dissolves. Pour the strained mixture through a funnel into a plastic bottle, without leaving any head room. If the liquid doesn't fill the bottle, you probably lost some to the strainer. Simply fill to the top with plain warm water. Fasten the cap and let it sit out in a warm place in your kitchen for 24 to 48 hours. When the bottle feels hard to the touch and begins to bulge, refrigerate it. The carbonation should last at least 1 week after opening.

ALMOND MILK

Homemade almond milk is so easy to make and is so fresh tasting compared to packaged almond milk. It is great in smoothies, on Granola Your Way (page 175) or whole-grain porridges (see page 179), heated up for hot chocolate, or simply enjoyed as a beverage, sweetened with a little agave syrup or honey and a dash of vanilla extract. The more powerful your blender, the better the results. I make almond milk with an old thrift-store blender just fine, but I have to strain it well. No need to discard the spent almond pulp. Spread it out thinly on a cookie sheet and dry it in a 200-degree-F oven for 6 to 8 hours. Sprinkle it over yogurt or porridge or add to muffins or cookies. You can freeze the dried pulp and use it over time.

TIME REQUIRED: *20 minutes active; 8 to 12 hours passive*
YIELD: *about 5 cups*

2 cups (about 8 ounces) whole raw almonds

Soak the almonds in 8 cups water overnight or for up to 15 hours in a bowl in the refrigerator. Puree the almonds, using all of the water, in batches in a blender and strain through a medium-mesh strainer. Pour into a jar or bottle, seal, and refrigerate. The milk will keep, refrigerated, for 5 days.

Chill and shake before serving. Sweeten and embellish to taste with vanilla, cinnamon, honey, maple syrup, sugar, or agave syrup.

HORCHATA

There are many variations of this drink, depending on the country of origin. I have heard that the original version came from Spain and is made with tiger nuts (sometimes called chufas), which are actually rhizomes rather than nuts. Some Central American versions contain different kinds of nuts and seeds, like pumpkin seeds. I've seen Mexican recipes that contain almonds and milk, instead of water. I settled on this plain rice version made with water, because horchata was probably originally a simple beverage made by people without access to refrigeration. Plus, it's so creamy and delicious as is, why waste precious dairy?

Most versions contain sugar, but I think agave syrup is excellent here because it dissolves readily in room-temperature liquids. If you want to make this with sugar, you should heat the rice beverage after you blend it so the sugar will dissolve. Depending on your taste, you'll want to use more sugar than the agave syrup called for here because it is generally 25 percent less sweet than agave syrup. This drink is wonderfully refreshing with spicy food.

TIME REQUIRED: *30 to 40 minutes active; 12 to 14 hours passive*
YIELD: *2 quarts*

2 cups long-grain white rice

1 vanilla bean

One 2-inch cinnamon stick

¼ to ⅓ cup agave syrup

Ground cinnamon for garnish (optional)

In a food processor or spice grinder, grind the rice to as fine a powder as possible. A spice grinder will do a better job much faster, but you'll have to do it in multiple batches. A good food processor with a sharp blade will do the job in about 10 minutes. Transfer to a large bowl, and add 8 cups water.

Split the vanilla bean lengthwise and, with the dull edge of a paring knife, scrape the seeds into the watery rice. Add the scraped bean hull and the cinnamon stick. Stir, cover, and refrigerate for 12 to 14 hours.

Remove the vanilla bean hull and cinnamon stick and process the rice mixture in a food processor or blender. Use whichever one has the sharpest blades and most powerful motor. Strain the mixture through a fine-mesh strainer, such as a chinoise (the cone-shaped, very fine mesh strainers used in restaurants). If you don't own one of these quite expensive implements, strain it through a regular strainer lined with a coffee filter. Stir and taste. It will be a little bit grainy, but if it's unpleasantly so, strain again. The outcome depends so much on the efficiency of your particular appliances and strainers, so experimentation is necessary.

Measure the resulting liquid. You should have between 7 and 8 cups. Add water to bring the volume up to 8 cups. Stir in agave syrup to taste. Pour it into bottles or jars and refrigerate for up to 5 days. Shake before serving. You may want to add a little ground cinnamon to garnish each serving.

HIBISCUS TEA

Called jamaica *(ha-MY-cuh) in Spanish, this ruby-hued drink is made from the flower of the hibiscus plant and is packed with vitamin C. Steeped in water and sweetened to tame its tartness, this is both refreshing and festive on a hot day, making it a great drink for a party. It's commonly served in Mexico, unadorned, but at Carrie Brown's Jimtown Store in California, where I first learned to make it, it's embellished with citrus, cinnamon, cloves, and cardamom. The amount of sugar is adjustable to taste, and I encourage experimentation with a few sprigs of mint or lemon verbena, a shot of citrus, or a measure of bubbly water. It's also great for a drink mixer with vodka or gin. Dried hibiscus flowers are widely available in Latin American groceries, health food stores, and specialty groceries.*

TIME REQUIRED: *10 minutes active; 10 minutes passive*
YIELD: *makes 1 gallon*

2 heaping cups dried hibiscus flowers

1 cup sugar

2 plain organic black tea bags (optional)

In a large pot, bring 1 gallon water to a boil. Turn off the heat, add the hibiscus flowers and sugar, and stir to dissolve the sugar. Add the tea (if using), and let it steep until it cools to room temperature. Strain carefully (it will stain!) and refrigerate for up to 1 week. Serve over ice, plain, or with one of the embellishments noted above.

Sources and Further Reading

Following are sources for those items that I feel are essential to the kitchen as well as any difficult-to-find cultures and other items that I have talked about in this book. I always try to look locally whenever possible so as to support my community and lower my impact on the environment, but I recognize that it isn't always possible to find some of the items here in all areas of the country. Following the sources for equipment and ingredients. I've included recommended books and Web sites for further information on some of the techniques in this book such as canning, fermenting, and culturing.

SOURCES

ALEPPO PEPPER

The Spice House
www.thespicehouse.com

BEER YEASTS FOR SOFT DRINKS

The Beverage People
www.thebeveragepeople.com

Oak Barrel Winecraft
www.oakbarrel.com

BONITO FLAKES

Eden Foods
www.edenfoods.com

Sushi and Japanese Market
www.shop.sushiandjapanesemarket.com

CAST-IRON PANS

Lodge Manufacturing Co.
www.lodgemfg.com

CERAMIC CLAY BAKERS

Breadtopia
www.breadtopia.com

CHEESEMAKING CULTURES
AND EQUIPMENT

The Beverage People
www.thebeveragepeople.com

New England Cheesemaking Supply Company
www.cheesemaking.com

DOMESTIC OLIVE OIL

California Olive Oil Council
www.cooc.com

The American Olive Oil Source
www.oliveoilsource.com

KOMBUCHA CULTURES

Anahata Balance
anahatabalance.com/store.html

Cultures for Health
www.culturesforhealth.com

KOREAN CRUSHED RED PEPPER

koaMart
www.koamart.com

PASTA MACHINES

Chef Depot
www.chefdepot.net

PIZZA PEEL AND STONE

Breadtopia—standard peels and
Exo superpeel
www.breadtopia.com

Sur la Table
www.surlatable.com

Zanesville Pottery
www.zanesvillepottery.com

**SEA VEGETABLES: KOMBU, NORI,
WAKAME**

Eden Foods
www.edenfoods.com

Mendocino Sea Vegetable Company
www.seaweed.net

True Foods Market
www.truefoodsmarket.com

SUSTAINABLE SEAFOOD CARDS

Blue Ocean Institute—searchable
directory, downloadable guides
*www.blueocean.org/seafood/
seafood-guide*

Environmental Defense Fund—downloadable seafood and sushi guides and
substitutions for red-listed species
www.edf.org

Monterey Bay Aquarium—searchable
directory, iPhone app, and downloadable guides by region
www.montereybayaquarium.org

TORTILLA PRESSES

Greenfeet
www.greenfeet.com

Mex Grocer
www.mexgrocer.com

VINEGAR CROCKS

Barkingside Co.
www.barkingside.com

Brew Beer
www.brewbeer.cc

Oak Barrel Winecraft
www.oakbarrel.com

Wine Guy Supply
www.shop.wineguysupply.com

VINEGAR MOTHERS

Local Harvest
www.localharvest.org

READING RECOMMENDATIONS

GENERAL

Bubel, Mike, and Nancy Bubel. *Root Cellaring: Natural Cold Storage of Fruits and Vegetables.* North Adams, MA: Storey Publishing, 1991.

Carroll, Ricki. *Home Cheese Making: Recipes for 75 Delicious Cheeses.* North Adams, MA: Storey Publishing, 2002.

Coyne, Kelly, and Erik Knutzen. *The Urban Homestead: Your Guide to Self-Sufficient Living in the Heart of the City.* Port Townsend, WA: Process Media, 2008.

Fallon, Sally. *Nourishing Traditions: The Cookbook that Challenges Politically Correct Nutrition and the Diet Dictocrats.* Revised Second Edition. Washington, DC: NewTrends Publishing, Inc., 2001.

The Gardeners and Farmers of Centre Terre Vivante. *Preserving Food Without Freezing or Canning: Traditional Techniques Using Salt, Oil, Sugar, Alcohol, Vinegar, Drying, Cold Storage, and Lactic Fermentation.* Foreword by Deborah Madison. White River Junction, VT: Chelsea Green Publishing, 1999.

Katz, Sandor Elix. *Wild Fermentation: The Flavor, Nutrition, and Craft of Live-Culture Foods.* Foreword by Sally Fallon. White River Junction, VT: Chelsea Green Publishing, 2003.

Morash, Marian. *The Victory Garden Cookbook.* New York: Alfred A. Knopf, Inc., 1982. (Out of print; find used copies on BetterWorldBooks.com, eBay.com, or Amazon.com)

Prentice, Jessica. *Full Moon Feast: Food and the Hunger for Connection.* Foreword by Deborah Madison. White River Junction, VT: Chelsea Green Publishing, 2006.

PET FOOD

Billinghurst, Ian, DVM. *The BARF Diet*. 4th Ed.: SOS Printing Pty Ltd., 2001.

Nestle, Marion. *Pet Food Politics: The Chihuahua in the Coal Mine*. Berkeley, CA: University of California Press, 2008.

Pitcairn, Richard H., DVM, PhD, and Susan Hubble Pitcairn. *Dr. Pitcairn's Complete Guide to Natural Health for Dogs and Cats*. 3rd Ed. New York: Rodale, 1982.

CANNING BOOKS WITH CHARTS

Devine, Lauren, and Judi Kingry, eds. *Ball Complete Book of Home Preserving*. Toronto, ON, Canada: Robert Rose, 2006.

Jarden Home Brands. *Ball Blue Book of Preserving*. 100th Anniversary Ed. Muncie, IN: Alltrista Consumer Products, 2004.

Rodale Food Center, and Susan McClure, eds. *Preserving Summer's Bounty*. Emmaus, PA: Rodale Press, 1990.

HELPFUL WEB SITES

Angelic Organics—Vegetable Storage Section
www.angelicorganics.com

Canning Processing Charts
www.scribd.com/doc/13902942/Canning-Processing-Charts

Fankhauser's Cheese Page
biology.clc.uc.edu/fankhauser/Cheese/CHEESE.HTML

Lists of farms where you can pick your own fruit, with canning advice
www.pickyourown.org

Mother Earth News
www.motherearthnews.com

Acknowledgments

First off, there are a few people without whom this book would never exist. I have to thank Susan Fleming, who gave me the confidence to think book-size big when I first conceived of this concept as a series of blog posts (and for supporting me throughout the process). Thanks to Raquel Dadomo and Haven Bourque, for reading the proposal with critical, but constructive, eyes and helping me get it off my computer and over to Chronicle Books. Thanks also to my Aunt Mil and all my other cooking relatives, for giving me the curiosity to investigate how things work in the kitchen, and for sharing the family recipes! Thanks to Jeff Fleming and Alice Grubb, for sharing the plum harvest.

I'm grateful to Bill LeBlond and all the folks at Chronicle Books for seeing the potential of this book and letting me run wild with the idea, while helping me shape it into what you see here. Especially Sarah Billingsley, for being always on the ball, and super to work with; Peter Perez, for his marketing genius and great ideas; designer Suzanne LaGasa, for her excitement about the project, her talent, and willingness to listen to my vision; and copy editor Ann Rolke, for smoothing out the rough edges, while leaving the essence of the book intact.

Thanks to Michael Straus and Haven Bourque at Straus Communications, and Sara Ost, my editor at EcoSalon.com, for their flexibility and generosity in giving me the time and space to work on this project. Thanks to the Cribari family, Eduardo Morell, and Rachel Cole, for sharing their specialized talents, knowledge, and recipes. Thanks to Emunah Hauser, for sleuthing out the sources.

Sara Remington, not only are your photos the most gorgeous ever, but you know how to make grueling work fun and put together a crack team of superpeople! I can't think of anyone I'd rather work with. Thanks to Kami Bremyer, prop stylist extraordinaire, for channeling my style perfectly based on a phone call and a few snapshots; to Nani Steele, for making the food look irresistible; to Stacy Ventura, for keeping us all fueled and for making it all run. Thanks to all of you for making five days of intense cooking and shooting a total blast.

Thanks to the friends who came to the shoot and helped. Thanks to the parents and kids who modeled: Suzie Wong and Mia Shao; Day Darmet, Florence Raynaud, and Chance; Nishanga Bliss and Milo; Sonya and Benjamin Philip and Beatrice; the neighbor kids, Rajvi and Anvi; and to Cameron and Henry and Susan Fleming for the kid wrangling.

There's a lot of cooking and eating that goes into a cookbook, which sometimes means eating the same thing over and over again, or being invited to dinner only to have to do dishes, not fed until 10 P.M., and served a bunch of dishes that don't go together by an exhausted, cranky host. Thanks to all the friends and family who continued to accept invitations to evenings that sometimes amounted to "no-host dinners": Bailey, Marcia, Christina, Oliver, Nishanga, Mike, Celia, Paula, and my sisters, Valerie Long and Vicki Rogers. And thanks to Susan, for all the dishwashing.

Recipe testers are really the key to a cookbook that is a pleasure to use. I can't thank you all enough for your efforts and great feedback: Parag Mody, Molly Watson, Juliet Glass, Bailey Foster, Vicki Rogers, Renee Perry, Megan Launer, and Susan Weber.

I am lucky to have the support and friendship of so many people. I hope I haven't left anyone out.

Index

TABLE OF EQUIVALENTS

The exact equivalents in the following table have been rounded for convenience.

LIQUID/DRY MEASURES

U.S.	METRIC
¼ teaspoon	1.25 milliliters
½ teaspoon	2.5 milliliters
1 teaspoon	5 milliliters
1 tablespoon (3 teaspoons)	15 milliliters
1 fluid ounce (2 tablespoons)	30 milliliters
¼ cup	60 milliliters
⅓ cup	80 milliliters
½ cup	120 milliliters
1 cup	240 milliliters
1 pint (2 cups)	480 milliliters
1 quart (4 cups, 32 ounces)	960 milliliters
1 gallon (4 quarts)	3.84 liters
1 ounce (by weight)	28 grams
1 pound	454 grams
2.2 pounds	1 kilogram

LENGTH

U.S.	METRIC
⅛ inch	3 millimeters
¼ inch	6 millimeters
½ inch	12 millimeters
1 inch	2.5 centimeters

OVEN TEMPERATURES

FAHRENHEIT	CELSUIS	GAS
250	120	½
275	140	1
300	150	2
325	160	3
350	180	4
375	190	5
400	200	6
425	220	7
450	230	8
475	240	9
500	260	10